INDIAN VEGETARIAN COOKING

· ·

AT YOUR HOUSE

by Sunetra Humbad and
Amy Schafer Boger, M.D.

Book Publishing Company · Summertown, TN 38483

Cover and interior design by Sheryl Karas
Illustrations by Jerry Lee Hutchens

Printed in the United States by Book Publishing Co.
PO Box 99
Summertown, TN 38483

ISBN 1-57067-004-8

Humbad, Sunetra, 1953-
    Indian vegetarian cooking at your house / Sunetra Humbad and
Amy Schafer Boger
        p.   cm.
    Includes index.
    ISBN 1-57067-004-8
    1. Vegetarian cookery. 2. Cookery, Indic.   I. Boger, Amy
    Schafer, 1955-   . II. Title
    TX837.H795   1955
641.5'636--dc20   94-44368
                                                        CIP

Calculations for the nutritional analyses in this book are based on the
average number of servings listed with the recipes and the average
amount of an ingredient, if a range is called for. Calculations for fat
content are rounded up to the nearest tenth of a gram; other calculations are rounded up to the nearest gram. If two options for an
ingredient are listed, the first one is used. Not included are optional
ingredients, serving suggestions, or fat used for frying, unless the
amount of fat is specified in the recipe.

CONTENTS

INTRODUCTION

WHO WE ARE: SUNETRA'S STORY

I was born in a small town called Aland, near Gulbarga, about half-way between Bangalore and Bombay, in the Southern part of India. Where I grew up, vegetarianism was part of our religion. We were taught never to kill a living being, for food or for any other reason. This was difficult sometimes, as when a poisonous lizard came into the house or when we were faced with annoying insects, but it is what we believed. I remember that it was a time of great distress for my father when, one day, he accidentally struck and killed a chicken with his car. After that, he would not drive any more.

I grew up in a wealthy household, not needing to do daily cooking. I observed my mother, an excellent cook, but I did not like to cook, because it seemed to be too much trouble. I especially disliked making chapatis, because I thought they took too much time to prepare. My mother said that my chapatis looked like maps of India, because they were never round. My family worried that when I left their home, I would not be able to take care of my new family.

For the first few years of my marriage, I continued not to cook very much. My mother frequently sent me food that she had prepared. I stayed with my mother or with my mother-in-law for the last part of pregnancy and the first months after delivery, as is our custom. As a new mother, I was not expected to share in the cooking.

Then, fifteen years ago, I moved to the United States with my husband (who was then a student at MIT) and two small sons. I found myself responsible for the tasks that my mother, aunts, and servants had done for my family in India, including the cooking. My sisters-in-law helped by sending written recipes, and I also had the memories of my mother's cooking. When I first began cooking, I used to burn myself all the time. I would also rush while slicing vegetables and cut myself. I would forget to add salt or add too much. Sometimes, I would forget that I had something on the stove, and I would burn it. Slowly, I became more experienced and skillful, but I still preferred uncomplicated cooking. It was at this time that I created my own versions of the traditional dishes I had known as a child, making them simpler to cook and using mostly foods easily available in the United States, but without changing the tastes which I remembered from India.

Now I am extremely comfortable in the kitchen. I have discovered that I enjoy cooking very much. Not only are my husband and four children well satisfied, but I have also taught many Indian cooking classes in the United States. The fact that I am so well known in my community for my cooking is amusing and pleasing to me, considering my beginnings as a cook. Every morning now, I make about 30 chapati (but I do not mind now, since much practice has made it easy and fast), and I make other foods for the day. My friends come to visit while I am cooking, to taste, to learn, or just to talk and share a cup of tea. Cooking Indian food is not hard, and it is fun. I hope that you enjoy learning these recipes and that you enjoy eating these foods "from my kitchen to yours."

WHO WE ARE: AMY'S STORY

I like to cook. I was raised cooking mostly traditional American foods, which I enjoy. I also like the taste of more exotic foods, but I am not the kind of cook who can create a new recipe out of her own head, especially when it comes to spices. I like to follow recipes, and I like to know that the result will be good when I try a new recipe. However, I do not buy cookbooks very often (or try recipes out of magazines) because these recipes are usually too time-consuming or don't turn out in my kitchen like they look in the book or magazine. When I had traveled as a teenager to England, I was introduced to the taste of Indian food in some of the many wonderful Indian restaurants in London. I thought of those foods as impossible to make myself, just to be remembered fondly and to be ordered if I could ever get to wonderful Indian restaurants again.

I like the idea of using less animal foods and more vegetable ones, for a variety of reasons. Both of my sisters are vegetarian. I tried vegetarianism in college, but my very conventional college dining hall usually had unsatisfactory and incomplete vegetarian options (often including chicken in the vegetarian dishes!). I returned to eating meat soon after, and many of my best recipes collected over the next years contained meat. In my mind, I wished I were eating a more vegetarian diet, but I didn't have many satisfactory dishes in my repertoire. As a medical student and pediatric resident, it did not matter what my recipes were like, since I rarely cooked (or slept). Later, as a pediatrician in private practice, my schedule became more bearable (relatively!), but my cooking experience remained limited. My husband said that he also was interested in eating more vegetables and non-animal foods. I wondered silently how he was going to like steamed vegetables and salads with beans on top, day after day.

I don't like to exercise, so it was pure luck that I happened to be at a health club at the right time to see a small, blue flyer for vegetarian Indian cooking classes by Sunetra Humbad. The idea of learning to cook Indian food, especially vegetarian Indian food, immediately appealed to me, but I was doubtful. I had never heard of

Sunetra nor tasted her cooking. Nevertheless, I called her to ask about her classes.

Sunetra was very gracious about my caution. She offered references and even invited me to her house to talk to her and to taste her food. The food was delicious. The visit and the refreshments persuaded me entirely that I should go ahead with the lessons, even before I gathered the glowing testimonials of people who knew her and her cooking. As I have come to know some of the people in the sphere of Sunetra's cooking, I am impressed by their diverse ethnic origin, education, occupation and age. Before meeting Sunetra, many of her friends never imagined that they would be relishing Indian snacks, luncheons, and dinners, nor that they could ever cook such food in their own homes.

At my first lesson, I learned to prepare five different Indian dishes, which together created a balanced meal. To my surprise and delight, when I tried to reproduce the dishes at my house, I had excellent results. Even my three young sons, typical finicky eaters, liked many of the dishes, especially the spiced rices and potato dishes. Sunetra, though teaching a cooking class for almost fifteen years, had never written down her recipes. With her encouragement, I soon began to translate my cooking class notes to a recipe format that I devised. I entered these recipes into our home computer and gave Sunetra and my classmates printed copies. Writing down the recipes in a consistent format often suggested questions and clarifications, and Sunetra would quickly set me straight when I had gotten something a bit wrong. Over the years, I eagerly attended as many lessons as Sunetra could give, until I had amassed the collection herein presented. Now my only problem is to get my husband to go out with me to an Indian restaurant. He says that he prefers my Indian cooking to any he can get out.

WHY YOU DON'T HAVE TO BE A VEGETARIAN TO USE THIS BOOK

Unlike many meat-eating animals, humans who eat meat actually have a mostly vegetarian diet. Even if someone eats meat at every single meal, most of the items on his plate are not meat-containing. Next to the chicken or steak, you will find various starches (pasta, rice, bread, potatoes, etc.), vegetables, salads, condiments, drinks and desserts. Many meat-eating people nowadays are also including meat-less meals in their menu-planning, for reasons including health, ethics, environmentalism, and economy. Using this cookbook does not require conversion to vegetarianism. People who want to continue to include meat in their diets can use these recipes as side dishes to "spice up" a meal or to make meat-less meals now and then.

WHY YOU DON'T HAVE TO BE FROM INDIA TO COOK AND ENJOY INDIAN FOOD

You do not need to be Indian to appreciate the taste of Indian food. Although most Americans do not routinely spice their food as often or as interestingly as Indians do, most of the flavors used are familiar to Americans. Peanuts, coconut, ginger, onion, garlic, cinnamon, cloves, and hot peppers are tastes known to all of us. While some of the combinations of spices might not be what you are used to, we think you will find them interesting and delightful. If you do not like hot pepper, you can reduce the amounts suggested in the recipes and still enjoy the wonderful tastes from the other spices and ingredients.

While these recipes are the 100% authentic productions of an Indian-born cook, her style of cooking uses available foods in as simple a way as possible. Without giving up the classic Indian taste, these recipes are uniquely accessible to American cooks. The cooking methods and techniques, with very few exceptions, require only the ability to chop vegetables, measure spices and other ingredients, and follow simple directions about the order in which to add the ingredients. A few of the Indian breads and a very few of the other recipes will invite you to learn how to roll something out or up, but even these skills will be somewhat familiar to people who bake breads or desserts.

You need not worry about kitchen utensils, either. If you have a sharp knife, spatula, saucepans, stirring spoons, a frying pan or griddle, measuring cups and spoons, rolling pin, deep fat frying pan or wok, candy thermometer, and a blender or food processor, you are all set to make almost every recipe in this book. Most of these dishes are cooked on top of the stove.

WHY INGREDIENTS ARE NOT A PROBLEM

Although this is classic Indian cooking, most of the recipes in this book can be made without a visit to an Indian grocery store. If you have a good supermarket near you and a health food, gourmet, or other specialty store within reach, you will have everything you need for most of these dishes. If you can get to an Indian store *occasionally*, you can fill in your few gaps. If you cannot get to an Indian store, some of them will mail ingredients out, which is especially useful for spices or other ingredients that you use a little at a time and that keep well. At the end of this book, we include a listing of Indian grocery stores (and other stores that carry spices, rices, and flours used in Indian cooking) across the United States and Canada.

Most of the recipes in this book use vegetables that you can find in any good supermarket or produce market in the North America, rather than Indian-type vegetables, which are a little different from the American varieties. Scan through a few recipes under the heading "fresh ingredients," and you will see mostly onion, tomato, garlic, ginger, coriander (also called cilantro—usually not hard to find and quite possible to freeze—see page 13), spinach, green beans, potatoes, eggplant, peas, and other common vegetables.

For starches, the ideal rice is long-grained basmati, best bought in an Indian store, but also available in most health food and gourmet stores, if not in your local supermarket. If you cannot get basmati rice, however, other rices can be used. For flour, some of these recipes call for all-purpose white flour; some call for Indian whole wheat flour (also called chapati flour), which is available in all Indian markets, but can be substituted, if necessary, with whole wheat pastry flour from health food stores. Even regular whole wheat flour would be OK, especially if mixed in even parts with white flour, but it is much coarser then the Indian kind. Chickpea flour (also called *besan*) and rice flour can often be found in health food stores and other ethnic markets.

The dried beans used in these recipes are usually readily available in supermarkets and health food stores: black-eyed peas, mung beans, yellow split peas, chickpeas, and lentils. A few of the recipes call for Indian beans (dals), like urrad dal or roasted Indian chickpeas, which would be found in some health food stores or which can be obtained at an Indian store or by mail. Sometimes such an ingredient can be left out or substituted by something easier to find. For example, when oily lentils (found mostly in Indian stores) are called for, you can always substitute other lentils or mung beans with good results.

Most of the spices used in these recipes are likewise usually easy to find: supermarkets carry cumin and coriander powders, hot red pepper powder, salt, sesame seeds, turmeric powder, and others. A few spices may require a trip to the gourmet or health food store, or maybe to an Indian store or mail order spice catalog. You do not need to buy spices frequently. Once you have a stock of the basic spices, you will not have to buy them again for a while.

HOW YOU CAN ADAPT THESE RECIPES FOR A LOW-FAT, LOW-SALT, OR OTHER SPECIAL DIET

We have reduced the amount of fat and oil wherever we could in these recipes without sacrificing the taste or texture of the dishes. The only source of cholesterol in Indian food is dairy products, and Indian cuisine is naturally lower in fats than most diets containing meat. Some of the desserts are quite rich, but they are usually eaten in very small portions. In addition, some of the desserts are low in fat: for example, Fruit Salad, Srikhand made with non-fat yogurt, and Roasted Chickpea Squares.

Some readers may wish to experiment with decreasing the oil and fat further, but the results may not be quite the same. Some of the individual recipes indicate that reducing the fats will detract from the flavor or texture of the dish.

For people who need or wish to limit their intake of salt and/or sugar, the suggested amounts in these recipes can usually be reduced by half, or possibly even more, without changing the taste of the dish substantially, especially if you are used to a low-salt or low-sugar taste already. Indeed, the bouquet of other spices will provide a vivid flavor even without salt.

Likewise, if your diet is gluten-free, you will find many recipes in this book without offending ingredients. If you are vegan, you will find many recipes that will satisfy you, though there are some which use dairy products.

A NOTE ABOUT PORTION SIZES

Traditionally, Indian food is served in small portions. Since a number of different dishes are usually made for a single meal, one does not take large portions of any one item. If a person wishes, however, he or she may certainly take seconds of any of the dishes. Because we wish to give an authentic picture of Indian food, we have retained the small portions in our listing with each recipe of the number of servings provided (traditional serving size). We do recognize that peoples' appetites differ, or you may want to serve only a few dishes at any one meal, so we also give the total yield for each recipe and invite our readers to serve themselves however they wish.

ABOUT CHUTNEYS

The concept of a chutney may seem unusual to many readers. Chutney is a strongly flavored condiment made from any of a wide variety of ingredients. It is used at a meal to spice up the other foods on the plate in much the same way that many Americans use ketchup. You can spoon the chutney onto one or more of the different foods on your plate; you can put a little pool of the chutney onto the plate, and dip foods into it; or you can mix the foods on your plate with the pool of chutney while you are eating. You can also spread chutney on bread as you would butter. A few chutneys are dry and can be sprinkled. Because chutney is used as a condiment, it is usually served in a portion size of a tablespoon or two. Serving a hot, spicy chutney is one way to allow different individuals to satisfy their particular tastes at the same meal.

HOW TO GET ORGANIZED TO COOK AN INDIAN MEAL

For a balanced meal, you might make one bean dish, two vegetable dishes, rice, and a chutney. In an Indian household, there would be a bread too.

One way to cook an Indian dish is to set out a bowl or two and a few little metal, ceramic, or plastic cups. (The plastic cups from applesauce or pudding snacks can be reused nicely for this.) If you want to make more than one dish, you might want to put a piece of paper naming the recipe next to each group of dishes and cups. Measure out the spices in little cups in the *groups* in which they are to be added, (otherwise you'll need too many little bowls).

Another possibility for the spices is to buy a traditional spice canister from an Indian store. These metal canisters are round and flat and have as inserts six or seven small metal cups which fit snugly into place. Into the little cups, an Indian cook will put her six or seven most-used spices; for example, cumin-coriander powder (see description at right), garam masala, Pav Bahji masala, turmeric powder, hot red pepper powder, seeds mixture (see description at right), cumin seeds, and a small container of hing. Since there are only small amounts of spices in each little bowl, the spices do not get stale or "mixed" despite the open cups. The little cups can be refilled now and then from larger containers which can be kept in a less convenient place. When spicing dishes, the cook can pull out most (or all) of the spices she needs all at once in the single container. Using a spice canister, and seasoning only one dish at a time, you might not have to pre-measure the spices in little cups.

Before you turn on the stove, chop the relevant vegetables and set them aside by their label in separate bowls. If two vegetables are to be added at the same time, put them in a bowl together. Some people cut up vegetables in a batch and freeze them, especially things like onion or hot pepper when a recipe might not call for the whole vegetable. Coriander leaves (cilantro) can be kept by chopping them and putting them in an ice cube tray with a very small amount of water to freeze into cubes; they will retain

Spice Mixes:

Cumin-Coriander Powder:
Combine equal amounts of cumin powder and coriander powder.

Seeds Mixture:
Combine one part each of cumin seeds and sesame seeds with two parts *black* mustard seeds.

their taste but not their texture, though this would not matter in a simmered dish. Another way we have simplified cooking from these recipes is by listing the ingredients both before and within each recipe. At the top of each recipe, you will see the list of ingredients divided into three categories: *Fresh Ingredients, Spices,* and *Other Ingredients* (usually staples or other foods that keep very well). This list can help you with your shopping, because once you have set up your kitchen for Indian cooking with a basic collection of spices, staples, and dried beans, you will usually only have to buy things from the fresh list on any particular occasion. (See *Pantry Set-up,* pg. 178.) Within each recipe, the ingredients are again listed in their entirety at the time when they are to be added. This arrangement avoids the confusion and annoyance of looking up at the ingredients list, down at the recipe, up at the list, and so on.

The total time for the preparation of an Indian meal from this book mostly depends on how many different dishes you wish to include, but the actual cooking of the dishes is almost always extremely simple. When cooking a dish, it is mainly a matter of emptying into a saucepan the contents of a few different bowls and cups in the right order and stirring. A few of these recipes take a little time or supervision on the stove, but most do not. An additional feature of this kind of cooking is that most of the dishes taste just as good as left-overs.

The tastes that can come out of a American kitchen with a few new spices, a few new ingredients, and these recipes are astounding. With only these few additions to your pantry, you can cook a wide variety of vegetarian dishes, using no meat, but supplying full nutritional benefits easily and flavorfully.

SUNETRA'S KITCHEN HINTS

- Put water in a pan before milk.
- Put salt in deep-frying oil to avert smoking.
- If there's too much salt in a dish, add ½ potato.
- If a food is too hot, add oil or peanuts.
- Hot pepper: always add to taste.
- Stock hot-pepper mixture (can keep in freezer for a short time): Grind together 1 fresh hot pepper, 1 clove garlic, 1 tsp cumin seeds, ½" fresh ginger, grated.
- Add a few drops of lime juice to rice cooking water to keep rice white and fluffy.
- Don't wash okra with water; just wipe with a damp cloth.
- If tomatoes, radishes, beets, or carrots get soft, crisp them by soaking overnight in salt water.
- To keep boiled potatoes white, add a few drops of lime juice to the cooking water.
- To keep cut apples white, wipe with lime juice.
- To get skin off garlic cloves, put a little oil in your palms, and rub clove between oily palms.
- To skin peanuts, put in a cloth bag or wrap securely in a cloth, rub gently, and tap on counter.
- When pan-roasting peanuts, rub in wet hands first, and they will be crunchier and tastier.
- Soak lemon in warm water for 3-4 minutes before using to make it juicier.
- After boiling milk, add water to the pan scrapings, and use that to make your rice.
- Storing coconut (or hing) in dal retards spoiling.
- Store cream of wheat in a plastic bag, slightly open—retards spoiling.
- To open a coconut, make a line with water, and crack open gently on floor.
- When a vegetable is in the refrigerator too long and goes dry, soak in lime juice mixed with cold water to freshen.
- When chopping onion, drop the chopped part into cold water to make it less irritating to the eyes.
- Potatoes are easiest to peel if you cook them first and then let them cool.

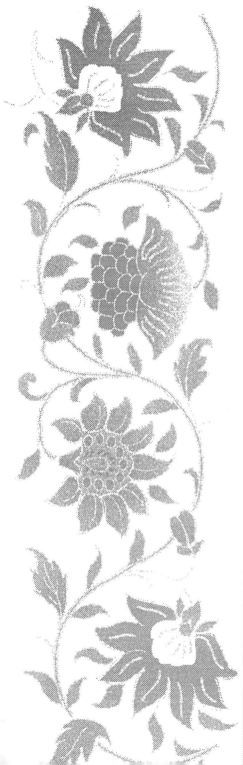

SOUPS, SNACKS & DRINKS

SOUPS

Lentil Soup 17
Flavored with spices and coconut

Lentil Vegetable Soup 20
With vegetables and rice

Peanut Soup 22
With crushed, roasted peanuts and spices

Yogurt Soup 23
With spices and yogurt

SNACKS

Chapati Chawada 24
Mix of seasoned chapatis and nuts

Shev 25
Spicy, fried morsels made of chickpea and rice flours

Peanut Snack Mix 26
With peanuts, roasted chickpeas, and spices

Salty Chirote 27
Spicy fried dough

Spicy Popcorn 28
Sweet and hot seasoned popcorn

Spicy Snack Mix 29
Seasoned puffed rice with peanuts and roasted chickpeas

DRINKS

Ginger Tea 30
Sweetened tea with milk, ginger, and spices

Indian Coffee 31
Sweetened coffee with milk, ginger, and spices

Sweet Lassi 32
Heavenly sweet, rich yogurt drink

Yogurt Lassi 33
Refreshing, savory yogurt drink

LENTIL SOUP

LENTIL SOUP FLAVORED WITH SPICES AND COCONUT

Makes 6 cups
(traditional serving = ⅓ cup)

*Per serving: Calories: 43,
Protein: 2 gm., Fat: 1.4 gm.,
Carbohydrates: 6 gm.*

• • • •

Fresh Ingredients
*garlic, ½ clove
onion, 1 cup
tomato, 1 medium
fresh green hot pepper, 2"
coriander leaves (cilantro),
    2 TBS*

Other Ingredients
*lentils, oily (or other),
    ½ cup, dry
salt, 1 tsp
vegetable oil, 1 TBS
brown sugar, 1 TBS
coconut, unsweetened,
    1 TBS*

Spices
*turmeric, 1 tsp
hing, pinch
seeds mixture, ½ tsp
Indian bay leaves, 4-5*

Rinse well and cook in 2 cups water till soft—about 30 minutes:

> **½ cup oily (or other) lentils (makes 1½ cups cooked)**

Place the lentils and their cooking liquid in a bowl with:

> **1 teaspoon turmeric**
> **1 teaspoon salt**

Mix with a rotary beater or in a blender or food processor until smooth.

Heat in a saucepan:

> **1 Tablespoon vegetable oil**

Add and sauté until the seeds pop:

> **pinch hing**
> **½ teaspoon cumin/mustard/sesame seed mix**
> **4-5 Indian bay leaves**
> **2 dried hot peppers (opt.)**

Add chopped vegetables and sauté until soft:

> **½ clove garlic, chopped**
> **1 cup onion, chopped**
> **1 medium tomato, chopped**
> **2 inches fresh, green hot pepper, chopped**
> **2 Tablespoons fresh coriander leaves (cilantro), chopped**

Stir in:

> **1 Tablespoon brown sugar**
> **1 Tablespoon unsweetened coconut**

(cont.)

Then add the powdered spices:

  1½ teaspoons cumin/coriander powder
  1 teaspoon hot red pepper powder (opt.)
  ½ teaspoon garam masala
  ½ teaspoon other masala (or more garam masala)

Add the lentil mixture and ⅔ cup water (or more) to make a thin paste or thick liquid; cook until heated through.

Spices (cont.)
(optional: dried hot peppers, 2)
cumin/coriander powder, 1½ tsp
(optional: hot red pepper powder, 1 tsp)
garam masala, 1 tsp or ½ tsp + ½ tsp any other masala

LENTIL VEGETABLE SOUP

Lᴇɴᴛɪʟ Sᴏᴜᴘ Wɪᴛʜ Vᴇɢᴇᴛᴀʙʟᴇ ᴀɴᴅ Rɪᴄᴇ

Makes about 6 cups
(traditional serving=⅓ cup)

*Per serving: Calories: 40 ,
Protein: 2 gm., Fat: 0.8 gm.,
Carbohydrates: 7 gm.*

• • • •

Fresh Ingredients
*butter, unsalted, 1 TBS
onion, 2½ TBS
garlic, 2 cloves
jalapeño pepper, ½
tomato, ½
celery, ½ cup
carrots, ½ cup
(optional: scallions, ¼ cup)
parsley, ½ cup
coriander leaves (cilantro),
  ½ TBS*

Other Ingredients
*salt, ½ TBS
lentils, brown (or orange),
  ½ cup uncooked
basmati rice, ½ cup uncooked
  (or 1 cup cooked)*
                        (cont.)

Have **1 cup cooked basmati rice** ready, or bring to a boil in a saucepan:
> **½ cup uncooked, rinsed basmati rice**
> **⅔ cup water**

Cover, turn the heat to low, and cook for 15-20 minutes, until the water is absorbed; set aside.

In a large saucepan, melt:
> **1 Tablespoon unsalted butter**

Add and sauté over moderate heat until softened:
> **2½ Tablepoons onion, chopped**
> **2 cloves garlic, chopped**
> **½ fresh jalapeño pepper, chopped**
> **½ tomato, chopped**
> **½ cup celery, finely chopped**
> **½ cup carrots, finely chopped**
> **¼ cup scallions, chopped (opt.)**

Add:
> **½ cup fresh parsley, chopped finely**
> **½ Tablespoon fresh coriander leaves (cilantro),
>   chopped**
> **½ Tablespoon salt**
> **½ teaspoon ground black pepper**
> **¼ teaspoon cumin/coriander powder**
> **2 cups water**

Now add:

½ cup uncooked, washed brown or "orange"
lentils

Simmer, uncovered, for about an hour. You will probably need to add about 1 more cup of water while cooking.

Before serving, add:

the cooked rice

Heat through and serve. This soup is also excellent without the rice.

Spices (cont.)
black pepper, ground, ½ tsp
cumin/coriander powder,
¼ tsp

PEANUT SOUP
SPICY SOUP WITH CRUSHED ROASTED PEANUTS

Makes 4 cups
(traditional serving = ⅓ cup)

*Per serving: Calories: 81,
Protein: 3 gm., Fat: 6.5 gm.,
Carbohydrates: 2 gm.*

• • • •

Fresh Ingredients
*coriander leaves (cilantro),
    2 TBS*

Other Ingredients
*peanuts, roasted, 1 cup
salt, 1 tsp
vegetable oil, 1 TBS*

Spices
*cumin/coriander powder,
    1 TBS
hot red pepper powder,
    1-2 tsp
turmeric, 1 tsp
garam masala, ½ tsp
hing, pinch
seeds mixture, 1 tsp*

Crush in a mortar and pestle, in a bag using a rolling pin, or briefly in a blender:
> **1 cup roasted peanuts**

Mix together with the peanuts in a bowl:
> **1 Tablespoon cumin/coriander powder**
> **1-2 teaspoons hot red pepper powder**
> **1 teaspoon turmeric**
> **1 teaspoon salt**
> **½ teaspoon garam masala**
> **2 Tablespoons fresh coriander leaves (cilantro), chopped**
> **3 cups water**

In a saucepan, heat:
> **1 Tablespoon vegetable oil**
> **pinch hing**
> **1 teaspoon cumin/mustard/sesame seed mixture**

When the seeds pop, add the peanut mixture. Bring to a boil, remove from heat, and serve.

This goes well with corn chapatis and stuffed onions.

YOGURT SOUP
Soup Flavored with Spices and Yogurt

Mix well with an egg beater:
>   1½ cup plain yogurt
>   1½ Tablespoons chickpea flour
>   ¾ teaspoon ginger powder

Mix in and set aside:
>   1½ teaspoon salt
>   2¼ cups water

Heat in a saucepan:
>   1½ teaspoons ghee (or unsweetened butter)

Add:
>   6-8 black mustard seeds
>   3-4 Indian bay leaves
>   7-9 fenugreek seeds
>   ⅓ teaspoon turmeric
>   3-4 slices fresh, hot green pepper (optional)
>   ¾ teaspoon fresh coriander leaves (cilantro),
>   chopped (optional)

Add the yogurt mixture to the spices in the saucepan, and heat, *stirring constantly* (or else the soup will separate). When the soup comes to a boil, immediately remove it from the heat, and serve.

Makes 3½–4 cups
(traditional serving=⅓ cup)

Per serving: Calories: 29 , Protein: 2 gm., Fat: 1 gm., Carbohydrates: 3 gm.

• • • •

Fresh Ingredients
*yogurt, plain, 1½ cup
(optional: fresh hot pepper, 3-4 slices)
(optional: coriander leaves [cilantro], ¾ tsp)*

Other Ingredients
*chickpea flour, 1½ TBS
salt, 1½ tsp
ghee, 1½ tsp (or unsweetened butter)*

Spices
*ginger powder, ¾ tsp
black mustard seeds, 6-8
Indian bay leaves, 3-4
fenugreek seeds, 7-9
turmeric, ⅓ tsp*

CHAPATI CHAWADA
SNACK MIX OF SEASONED CHAPATIS AND NUTS

Makes about 2¼ cups
(traditional serving = 3 TBS)

Per serving: Calories: 47,
Protein: 1 gm., Fat: 2.7 gm.,
Carbohydrates: 5 gm.

• • • •

Fresh Ingredients
chapatis, 2 cups (see pg. 64)
coriander leaves (cilantro),
5-6 leaves

Other Ingredients
roasted Indian chickpeas,
1 TBS
roasted peanuts, 1 TBS
sugar, 2 tsp
vegetable oil, 2 TBS
salt, ½ tsp

Spices
cumin/coriander powder,
1 tsp
turmeric powder, ½ tsp
hot red pepper powder,
⅓ tsp
garam masala, pinch
hing, tiny pinch
seeds mixture, pinch
Indian bay leaf, pinch
dried hot pepper, 1

In a bowl, mix:

>   2 cups dry chapatis, crumbled and crushed into
>   small pieces
>   1 Tablespoon roasted (small) Indian chickpeas
>   1 Tablespoon whole, roasted peanuts (Indian or
>   other variety)
>   2 teaspoons sugar
>   1 teaspoon coriander/cumin powder
>   ½ teaspoon salt
>   ½ teaspoon turmeric
>   ⅓ teaspoon hot red pepper powder
>   1 pinch garam masala

Heat in a saucepan:

>   2 Tablespoons vegetable oil
>   tiny pinch hing

Add:

>   1 pinch cumin/mustard/sesame seed mixture
>   1 pinch Indian bay leaf, crumbled
>   1 whole, dry, red hot pepper

Add:

>   the chapati mixture
>   5-6 fresh coriander leaves (cilantro)

Mix well over heat for a few minutes, and serve by itself as a
snack or with yogurt.

This is a good way to use left-over chapati.

SHEV
Spicy, Fried Morsels Made of Chickpea and Rice Flours

In a bowl, mix well:
- 1½ cups rice flour
- ½ cup chickpea flour
- 1½ Tablespoons roasted sesame seeds
- 1 Tablespoon cumin/coriander powder
- 3 Tablespoons vegetable oil
- 1½ teaspoons salt
- ½-1 teaspoon hot red pepper powder (or more to taste)
- ¾ teaspoon fresh coriander leaves (cilantro), chopped
- ½ teaspoon cumin seeds
- ½ teaspoon turmeric
- ¼ teaspoon oregano seeds (ajama)
- pinch hing

Add water bit by bit to make a soft dough, about ⅔ cup. Using a cookie press, spritz dough into flat, 1½"-2" wide spirals on waxed paper. Alternately, you can use a strong plastic freezer bag with a ⅜" hole snipped in one corner to squeeze out the spirals. In this case, be sure the dough is very soft so the bag won't break. Deep fry until brown and crispy.

Makes about 2½-3 dozen
(traditional serving = 2)

Per serving: Calories: 98, Protein: 2 gm., Fat: 3.3 gm., Carbohydrates: 15 gm.

• • • •

Fresh Ingredients
*coriander leaves (cilantro),
    ¾ tsp*

Other Ingredients
*rice flour, 1½ cups
chickpea flour, ½ cup
sesame seeds, roasted,
    1½ TBS
vegetable oil, 3 TBS, and for
    deep frying
salt, 1½ tsp*

Spices
*cumin/coriander powder,
    1 TBS
hot red pepper powder,
    ½-1 tsp
turmeric, ½ tsp
cumin seeds, ½ tsp
oregano seeds (ajama),
    ¼ tsp
hing, pinch*

PEANUT SNACK MIX
SEASONED SNACK MIX WITH PEANUTS AND ROASTED CHICKPEAS

Makes about 2 cups
(traditional serving = 3 TBS)

Per serving: Calories: 176,
Protein: 6 gm., Fat: 12 gm.,
Carbohydrates: 10 gm.

• • • •

Fresh Ingredients
coriander leaves (cilantro),
¼ cup
lemon (or lime) juice,
1½ TBS

Other Ingredients
roasted Indian chickpeas,
½ cup
roasted Indian or Spanish
peanuts, ½ cup
raw Indian or Spanish
peanuts, ½ cup
sugar, 1 tsp
salt, 1 tsp
vegetable oil, 1 tsp

Spices
garam masala, ½ tsp
hing, pinch

Mix together:

> ½ cup roasted Indian chickpeas
> ½ cup roasted peanuts (Indian, Spanish, or other variety)
> ½ cup raw peanuts (Indian, Spanish, or other variety)
> ¼ cup fresh coriander leaves (cilantro), minced
> 1½ Tablespoons lemon or lime juice
> 1 teaspoon sugar
> 1 teaspoon salt
> 1 teaspoon vegetable oil
> ½ teaspoon garam masala
> pinch hing

SALTY CHIROTE
SPICY FRIED DOUGH

To make the dough, mix in a bowl (or use leftover samosa dough):

> **1 cup white flour**
> **2 teaspoons rice flour**
> **4 teaspoons vegetable oil**
> **¼ teaspoon salt**

Add water gradually (about 2-3 Tablespoons) until the dough holds together; knead well. Roll into a ball and cover with a moist cloth. Let rest about 20 minutes.

Sprinkle on and knead in:

> **½ teaspoon oregano seeds (ajama)**
> **¼ teaspoon black numkin (opt.)**
> **salt to taste**

Roll into a circle 12 inches in diameter. Cut immediately into diamonds with lines about 1½" apart; deep fry until browned.

Makes about 4 dozen
(traditional serving = 2-3)

Per serving: Calories: 56, Protein: 1 gm., Fat: 3.7 gm., Carbohydrates: 5 gm.

• • • •

Fresh Ingredients

Other Ingredients
white flour, 1 cup
rice flour, 2 tsp
vegetable oil, 4 tsp, and for deep frying
salt, ¼ teaspoon and for sprinkling

Spices
oregano seeds (ajama), ½ tsp
(optional: black numkin, ¼ tsp)

Makes 5-6 cups
(traditional serving = ½ cup)

Per serving: Calories: 48,
Protein: 1 gm., Fat: 3.6 gm.,
Carbohydrates: 3 gm.

• • • •

Fresh Ingredients

Other Ingredients
vegetable oil, 3-4 TBS
popping corn, ¼ cup
sugar, ½ tsp
salt, ¼ tsp

Spices
turmeric, ¼ tsp
hot red pepper powder, pinch

SPICY POPCORN
SWEET AND HOT SEASONED POPCORN

In a heavy-bottomed, six-quart saucepan (or larger), place:
3-4 Tablespoons vegetable oil
several kernels popcorn

When the kernels pop, add all at once:
¼ cup popcorn kernels

Cover and pop, shaking frequently.

Pour the popped corn into large paper bag, and add:
½ teaspoon sugar
¼ teaspoon salt
¼ teaspoon turmeric
pinch hot red pepper powder

Shake and serve.

SPICY SNACK MIX

SEASONED PUFFED RICE WITH PEANUTS AND ROASTED CHICKPEAS

In a large saucepan, heat:
> **2½ Tablespoons vegetable oil**
> **pinch hing**
> **½ teaspoon cumin/mustard/sesame seed mixture**

When the seeds pop, add and roast in the pan:
> **¼ cup raw peanuts**

Next, add:
> **2½ Tablespoons roasted Indian chickpeas**
> **1 Tablespoon fresh coriander leaves (cilantro),**
> **chopped**

Remove from the heat, and add:
> **2-3 Indian bay leaves**
> **1½ teaspoons cumin/coriander powder**
> **½ teaspoon turmeric**
> **¼ teaspoon hot red pepper powder**
> **¼ teaspoon garam masala**

Now add:
> **2½-3 cups puffed rice**
> **2 teaspoons sugar**
> **1 teaspoon salt**

Mix very well and adjust spices to taste. You may add a small amount of popped popcorn, if you wish.

Makes 3¼ cups
(traditional serving = 3 TBS)

Per serving: Calories: 43, Protein: 1 gm., Fat: 2.9 gm., Carbohydrates: 3 gm.

• • • •

Fresh Ingredients
coriander leaves (cilantro),
  1 TBS

Other Ingredients
vegetable oil, 2½ TBS
peanuts, raw, ¼ cup
roasted Indian chickpeas,
  2½ TBS
puffed rice, 2½-3 cups
sugar, 2 tsp
salt, 1 tsp
(optional: popcorn, popped,
  small amount)

Spices
hing, pinch
seeds mixture, ½ tsp
Indian bay leaves, 2-3
cumin/coriander powder,
  1½ tsp
turmeric, ½ tsp
hot red pepper powder, ¼ tsp
garam masala, ¼ tsp

GINGER TEA
SWEETENED TEA, BREWED WITH MILK, GINGER, AND SPICES

Makes about 6 cups
(traditional serving = ¾ cup)

*Per serving: Calories: 76,
Protein: 3 gm., Fat: 2.9 gm.,
Carbohydrates: 9 gm.*

• • • •

Fresh Ingredients
*whole milk, 3 cups
fresh ginger, 1½ -3TBS*

Other Ingredients
sugar, 3 TBS

Spices
tea masala, 1½ tsp
tea bags, black tea, 9
Indian tea, loose, 1 TBS
(optional: mint leaves, 3)*

Loose tea from Indian groceries is much stronger than most tea sold in tea bags in this country. If you want a stronger tea, you can use 3 Tablespoons of loose Indian tea and omit the tea bags.

Mix in saucepan:
>   3 cups water
>   3 cups whole milk
>   3 Tablespoons sugar
>   1½-3 Tablespoons grated fresh ginger
>   1½ teaspoons tea masala*
>   contents of 9 tea bags
>   1 Tablespoon loose Indian tea
>   3 mint leaves (opt.)

Bring to a boil, cover, turn the heat to low, and simmer for about 2 minutes. Strain into a teapot, pitcher, or individual cups.

*To make tea masala, mix well together:
>   3 Tablespoons ginger powder
>   ½ Tablespoon clove powder
>   ½ Tablespoon black pepper powder
>   1 Tablespoon cinnamon powder
>   1 Tablespoon cardamom powder

You can save a batch of tea masala and use it over time—no need to make it fresh each time.

INDIAN COFFEE
SWEETENED COFFEE, BREWED WITH MILK, GINGER, AND SPICES

In a heavy saucepan, bring to a boil:

    3 cups whole milk
    3 cups water
    ⅓ cup sugar
    3 Tablespoons ground coffee beans,
        or 1½ Tablespoons instant coffee
    3 Tablespoons fresh grated ginger
    1½ teaspoons tea masala*

Cover, turn the heat to low, and simmer for about 2 minutes. Strain into a teapot, pitcher, or directly into cups.

*To make tea masala, mix well together:

    3 Tablespoons ginger powder
    ½ Tablespoon clove powder
    ½ Tablespoon black pepper powder
    1 Tablespoon cinnamon powder
    1 Tablespoon cardamom powder

You can save a batch of tea masala and use it over time—no need to make it fresh each time.

Makes about 6 cups
(traditional serving = ¾ cup)

Per serving: Calories: 102, Protein: 3 gm., Fat: 2.8 gm., Carbohydrates: 15 gm.

• • • •

Fresh Ingredients
whole milk, 3 cups
fresh ginger, 3 TBS

Other Ingredients
sugar, ⅓ cup
ground coffee beans, 3 TBS,
    or instant coffee, 1½ TBS

Spices
tea masala, 1½ tsp*

SWEET LASSI
HEAVENLY SWEET, RICH, YOGURT DRINK

Makes about 7 cups
(traditional serving = ¾ cup)

*Per serving: Calories: 226,
Protein: 4 gm., Fat: 11.8 gm.,
Carbohydrates: 24 gm.*

• • • •

Fresh Ingredients
*yogurt, whole milk, plain,
    4 cups
heavy cream, 1 cup*

Other Ingredients
*sugar, 1 cup
salt, 1 tsp*

Spices

Crush in a blender:
    4 cubes ice

Add and mix until frothy:
    4 cups plain, whole milk yogurt
    1 cup heavy cream
    1 cup sugar
    1 teaspoon salt
    2 cups water

YOGURT LASSI
REFRESHING, SAVORY YOGURT DRINK

In a blender or food processor, grind together:
> ½ jalapeño pepper, ground
> 1 clove garlic, ground
> ½ inch cube ginger, grated
> 1 Tablespoon fresh coriander leaves (cilantro),
>   chopped (opt.)

Add and blend together until frothy:
> 3 cups plain yogurt
> 2 teaspoons salt
> ¼ teaspoon cumin seeds
> 3½ cups cold water

You can also grind the first four ingredients in a mortar and pestle and beat with the remaining ingredients until frothy. Serve chilled.

Makes about 6½ cups
(traditional serving = ¾ cup)

Per serving: Calories: 52,
Protein: 3 gm., Fat: 2.5 gm.,
Carbohydrates: 4 gm.

• • • •

Fresh Ingredients
jalapeño pepper, ½ pepper
garlic, 1 clove
ginger, ½ inch cube
(optional: coriander leaves
(cilantro), 1 TBS)
yogurt, plain, 3 cups

Other Ingredients
salt, 2 tsp

Spices
cumin seeds, ¼ tsp

CHUTNEYS

APPLE BUTTER CHUTNEY

SWEET AND SPICY CHUTNEY MADE FROM APPLE BUTTER AND TAMARIND PASTE

Makes 3⅓ cups
(traditional serving = 1-2 tsp)

Per serving: Calories: 8, Protein: 0 gm., Fat: 0 gm., Carbohydrates: 2 gm.

• • • •

Fresh Ingredients

Other Ingredients
apple butter, 14 oz. jar
tamarind paste, 1 TBS
salt, ¼ tsp

Spices
cumin seeds, 1 TBS
ground black pepper,
  ¼-½ TBS

Roast in a dry skillet, stirring constantly for 2-3 minutes until lightly browned:
> **1 Tablespoon cumin seeds**

Grind the seeds in a food mill or blender.

Add to the blender or bowl, and mix or beat with the seed powder for 2 minutes:
> **1 (14 ounce) jar apple butter**
> **1¾ cups water**
> **1 Tablespoon tamarind (imli) paste (more or less to taste)**
> **¼-½ Tablespoon ground black pepper**
> **¼ teaspoon salt**

This chutney will keep in the refrigerator for a year and can also be frozen.

COCONUT CHUTNEY
SWEET CHUTNEY OF TOASTED COCONUT

Heat in a saucepan over medium heat:
> **2 Tablespoons vegetable oil**
> **tiny pinch hing**

Add:
> **1 teaspoon cumin/mustard/sesame seed mixture**
> **1 more teaspoon black mustard seeds**
> **1 more Tablespoon sesame seeds**

When the seeds start to pop, add:
> **1 Tablespoon fresh coriander leaves (cilantro), chopped**
> **1 teaspoon cumin/coriander powder**
> **½ teaspoon turmeric**
> **½ teaspoon hot red pepper powder**

Sauté briefly for 1-2 minutes, then turn off the heat.

Add:
> **1 cup unsweetened, shredded coconut**
> **1 Tablespoon sugar**
> **½ teaspoon salt**

Mix thoroughly.

Makes 1¼ cups
(traditional serving = 1-2 tsp)

Per serving: Calories: 46, Protein: 0 gm., Fat: 4 gm., Carbohydrates: 1 gm.

• • • •

Fresh Ingredients
coriander leaves (cilantro), 1 TBS

Other Ingredients
vegetable oil, 2 TBS
sesame seeds, 1 TBS
coconut, unsweetened, 1 cup
sugar, 1 TBS
salt, ½ tsp

Spices
hing, pinch
seeds mixture, 1 tsp
black mustard seeds, 1 tsp
cumin/coriander powder, 1 tsp
turmeric, ½ tsp
hot red pepper powder, ½ tsp

CORIANDER CHUTNEY
SAVORY CHUTNEY OF SPICED CORIANDER LEAVES (CILANTRO)

Makes 1 cup
(traditional serving = 1-2 tsp)

*Per serving: Calories: 7,
Protein: 0 gm., Fat: 0.6 gm.,
Carbohydrates: 0 gm.*

• • • •

Fresh Ingredients
*coriander leaves (cilantro),
  1 cup
ginger, 1 slice
garlic, 1 large clove
green chili pepper, 1*

Other Ingredients
*coconut, unsweetened,
  1½ TBS
peanuts, roasted, 1½ TBS
salt, ½ tsp*

Spices
cumin seeds, 1 tsp

Combine in a blender or food processor:
 1 cup (packed) fresh coriander leaves (cilantro)
 ½ cup water
 **1½ Tablespoons shredded, unsweetened
  coconut**
 1½ Tablespoons roasted peanuts
 1 teaspoon cumin seeds
 ½ teaspoon salt
 1 slice fresh ginger
 1 large clove garlic
 1 fresh green chili pepper

DOSA CHUTNEY
Yogurt Chutney with Coconut, Seeds, and Nuts

Grind together in a blender:

    3 Tablespoons unsweetened coconut
    2 Tablespoons fresh coriander leaves (cilantro), chopped
    1 Tablespoon roasted sesame seeds
    1 Tablespoon roasted peanuts
    1 Tablespoon roasted Indian chickpeas
    ½ teaspoon hot red pepper powder
    ½ teaspoon cumin seeds
    ½ teaspoon salt
    ¼ teaspoon tamarind paste
    1 clove garlic

Then mix in:

    6 Tablespoons water
    3 Tablespoons yogurt or sour cream

This goes well with *Dosa*, pg. 68, or *Idli Pancakes*, pg. 69.

Makes about 1 cup
(traditional serving = 1-2 tsp)

Per serving: Calories: 14, Protein: 0 gm., Fat: 1.1 gm., Carbohydrates: 1 gm.

• • • •

Fresh Ingredients
coriander leaves (cilantro), 2 TBS
garlic, 1 clove
yogurt (or sour cream), 3 TBS

Other Ingredients
sesame seeds, roasted, 1 TBS
peanuts, roasted, 1 TBS
Indian chickpeas, roasted, 1 TBS
coconut, unsweetened, 3 TBS
salt, ½ tsp
tamarind paste, ¼ tsp

Spices
hot red pepper powder, ½ tsp
cumin seeds, ½ tsp

GARLIC CHUTNEY

HOT AND STRONG CHUTNEY, MOSTLY OF GARLIC

Makes about ½ cup
(traditional serving = 1-2 tsp)

*Per serving: Calories: 33 ,
Protein: 0 gm., Fat: 2.6 gm.,
Carbohydrates: 2 gm.*

• • • •

Fresh Ingredients
garlic, 16 whole cloves

Other Ingredients
*coconut, unsweetened,
  4-6 TBS
salt, 2 tsp*

Spices
*cumin seeds, 2 tsp
paprika, 2 tsp
hot red pepper powder,
  ½-1 tsp
paprika, 2 tsp*

Grind together in the blender:
4-6 Tablespoons shredded unsweetened coconut
2 teaspoons cumin seeds
2 teaspoons paprika
2 teaspoons salt
½-1 teaspoon hot red pepper powder
16 whole cloves garlic

If you find the chutney too hot after you've added the hot pepper powder, you can add some oil to make it milder again.

This chutney is especially good mixed with yogurt and spread on paratha, chapati, etc. It is also good mixed with butter in a sandwich.

GREEN TOMATO CHUTNEY
Chutney of Cooked, Spiced Green Tomatoes

Cut small and sauté in a dry skillet over medium flame until fairly dry:

> **4 medium green tomatoes**

Add:

> **2 Tablespoons fresh coriander leaves (cilantro), chopped**
> **1½ Tablespoons vegetable oil**
> **1 teaspoon cumin seeds**
> **½ clove garlic, chopped**
> **½ fresh, hot green pepper**

Continue to sauté until the tomatoes are lightly browned.

Add:

> **1 Tablespoon whole roasted peanuts**
> **1 teaspoon sesame seeds**
> **1 teaspoon salt**

Continue to sauté until the tomatoes are browned and soft. Remove the mixture from the pan, and grind it coarsely in a blender.

In the same skillet, heat:

> **1 Tablespoon vegetable oil**
> **pinch hing**
> **¼ teaspoon cumin/mustard/sesame seed mixture**
> **2 Indian bay leaves**

When the seeds pop, add the blender mixture and stir briefly. If you find the chutney too hot, you can add brown sugar to make it milder.

Makes 1½-2 cups
(traditional serving = 1-2 tsp)

Per serving: Calories: 8, Protein: 0 gm., Fat: 0.7 gm., Carbohydrates: 0 gm.

• • • •

Fresh Ingredients
green tomatoes, 4 medium
coriander leaves (cilantro), 2 TBS
garlic, ½ clove
hot green pepper, ½

Other Ingredients
vegetable oil, 2½ TBS
peanuts, roasted, 1 TBS
sesame seeds, 1 tsp
salt, 1 tsp
(optional: brown sugar to taste)

Spices
cumin seeds, 1 tsp
hing, pinch
seeds mixture, ¼ tsp
Indian bay leaves, 2

HOT PEPPER CHUTNEY
Very Hot Chutney, Mostly of Cooked Hot Peppers

Makes 1 cup
(traditional serving = 1-2 tsp)

Per serving: Calories: 23,
Protein: 0 gm., Fat: 2.2 gm.,
Carbohydrates: 0 gm.

• • • •

Fresh Ingredients
hot green peppers, 9 peppers
coriander leaves (cilantro),
  2 TBS
garlic, ½ clove

Other Ingredients
vegetable oil, ⅓ cup
salt, 1 tsp
peanuts, roasted, 5 (or more
  to taste)

Spices
cumin seeds, 1 tsp
fenugreek seeds, pinch
hing, pinch
seeds mixture, ¼ tsp

Sauté until browned and soft:
> **⅓ cup vegetable oil**
> **9 hot green peppers, cut into large pieces**
> **(with seeds)**

If you want to reduce the oil or are sensitive to the cooking vapors emitted from sautéing hot peppers, you can roast the peppers with a little vegetable oil in a covered pan in a 375° oven for 45-60 minutes until browned.

When the peppers are browned, add and sauté or bake for 10 more minutes:
> **2 Tablespoons fresh coriander leaves (cilantro),**
>   **chopped**
> **1 teaspoon cumin seeds**
> **½ clove garlic, cut into large pieces**

Remove the pepper mixture from the pan with a slotted spoon: save the oil in the pan.

Place the pepper mixture in a blender, and add:
> **1 teaspoon salt**
> **5 roasted peanuts (more peanuts for milder chutney)**
> **pinch fenugreek seeds**

Grind into a coarse paste.

Reheat the oil in the pan with:
> **pinch hing**
> **¼ teaspoon cumin/mustard/sesame seed mixture**

When the seeds pop, add the blender mixture and stir briefly.

MANGO CHUTNEY
CHUTNEY OF SPICED, GREEN MANGOES

Mix together in a blender into a coarse paste:

2 small or 1 large hard (unripe) mangoes (or apples), chopped into chunks (about 2 cups)
1 Tablespoon roasted peanuts
1 Tablespoon brown sugar (or more to taste)
1 Tablespoon fresh coriander leaves (cilantro)
1 teaspoon coriander seeds
1 teaspoon cumin seeds
1 teaspoon salt (or to taste)
1 teaspoon hot red pepper powder
sugar to taste

Heat in a saucepan until the seeds pop:

1 Tablespoon vegetable oil
pinch hing
½ teaspoon cumin/mustard/sesame seed mixture

Stir the oil mixture into the mango mixture.

Makes about 1¼ cups
(traditional serving = 1-2 tsp)

Per serving: Calories: 10, Protein: 0 gm., Fat: 0.4 gm., Carbohydrates: 1 gm.

• • • •

Fresh Ingredients
mangoes, unripe, 2 small or 1 large
coriander leaves (cilantro), 1 TBS

Other Ingredients
peanuts, roasted, 1 TBS
brown sugar, 1 TBS (or more to taste)
salt, 1 tsp (or to taste)
vegetable oil, 1 TBS

Spices
coriander seeds, 1 tsp
cumin seeds, 1 tsp
hot red pepper powder, 1 tsp
hing, a pinch
seeds mixture, ½ tsp

ONION CHUTNEY

SIMPLE CHUTNEY OF MILDLY SPICED RAW ONIONS

Makes about 1 cup
(traditional serving = 1-2 tsp)

Per serving: Calories: 2,
Protein: 0 gm., Fat: 0 gm.,
Carbohydrates: 0 gm.

• • • •

Fresh Ingredients
onions, 1 cup

Other Ingredients
tomato ketchup, 1 tsp
white vinegar, 1 tsp
salt, ½ tsp

Spices
paprika, 1 tsp
hot red pepper powder, ½ tsp
cumin/coriander powder,
* ¼ tsp*

Mix together in a bowl:
> **1 cup onions, chopped**
> **1 teaspoon paprika**
> **1 teaspoon tomato ketchup**
> **1 teaspoon white vinegar**
> **½ teaspoon salt**
> **½ teaspoon hot red pepper powder**
> **¼ teaspoon cumin/coriander powder**

PEANUT CHUTNEY
SIMPLE CHUTNEY OF SPICED, CRUSHED PEANUTS

In a blender (or mortar and pestle) place:
> 1 cup roasted peanuts (Indian or any other variety)
> 2 teaspoons cumin seeds
> 2 teaspoons coriander seeds
> ½-1 teaspoon hot red pepper powder
> 1 teaspoon salt
> 1 clove garlic

Grind together in a blender or with a mortar and pestle (which gives you a consistency more like peanut butter—the blender mixture will be dry and crumbly).

This can be served drizzled with oil.

Makes 1⅓ cups
(traditional serving = 1-2 tsp)

Per serving: Calories: 20, Protein: 1 gm., Fat: 1.5 gm., Carbohydrates: 1 gm.

• • • •

Fresh Ingredients
garlic, 1 clove

Other Ingredients
peanuts, roasted, (Indian or any other variety) 1 cup
salt, 1 tsp

Spices
cumin seeds, 2 tsp
coriander seeds, 2 tsp
hot red pepper powder, ½-1 tsp

TAMARIND-DATE CHUTNEY
SWEET CHUTNEY OF DATES WITH TAMARIND PASTE

Makes 2 ¾ cups
(traditional serving = 1-2 tsp)

*Per serving: Calories: 7,
Protein: 0 gm., Fat: 0 gm.,
Carbohydrates: 2 gm.*

• • • •

Fresh Ingredients

Other Ingredients
*dates, 8 ounces (by weight)
tamarind paste, 1 TBS
salt, ½ tsp*

Spices
*cumin seeds, 1 TBS
dried hot peppers, 3-4*

In a skillet, dry roast, stirring constantly for about 2-3 minutes, until lightly browned:
> **1 Tablespoon cumin seeds**

Puree together in a blender:
> **8 ounces (1½ cups) pitted dates, coarsely chopped**
> **1 cup water**
> **1 Tablespoon tamarind paste**
> **½ teaspoon salt**
> **3-4 dried hot peppers**
> **the roasted cumin seeds**

Check the thickness and add more water to give it the consistency of heavy cream—about 1½ more cups. You can add more sugar if you think it's not sweet enough.

This will keep in the refrigerator up to 6 months; thin it with water as necessary.

This chutney goes very well with *Samosa*, pg. 73.

TAMARIND-SUGAR CHUTNEY
SWEET CHUTNEY OF TAMARIND PASTE WITH TWO SUGARS

You might want to use a larger portion of this sweet chutney than some of the stronger chutneys in this book.

Heat in a saucepan:
1 cup water
½ cup white sugar
½ cup brown sugar
1 Tablespoon tamarind paste

Bring to a boil and simmer until the sugar is dissolved, about 5 minutes.

In a blender, grind to a powder:
1 teaspoon roasted chickpeas

Add and blend:
1 Tablespoon fresh coriander leaves (cilantro), chopped
1 teaspoon roasted peanuts
¼ teaspoon hot red pepper powder
¼ teaspoon salt

Add the peanut mixture to the sweet liquid. Serve in small bowls or cups for dipping, or for pouring over *Khamong Dhokla*, pg. 106.

Makes about 2 cups
(traditional serving = 1-2 TBS)

Per serving: Calories: 10, Protein: 0 gm., Fat: 0 gm., Carbohydrates: 2 gm.

• • • •

Fresh Ingredients
coriander leaves (cilantro), 1 TBS

Other Ingredients
white sugar, ½ cup
brown sugar, ½ cup
tamarind paste, 1 TBS
chickpeas, roasted, 1 tsp
peanuts, roasted, 1 tsp
salt, ¼ tsp

Spices
hot red pepper powder, ¼ tsp

YOGURT CHUTNEY
Spicy Chutney of Yogurt With Peanuts

Makes 1½ cups
(traditional serving = 1-2 tsp)

*Per serving: Calories: 5,
Protein: 0 gm., Fat: 0.4 gm.,
Carbohydrates: 0 gm.*

• • • •

Fresh Ingredients
*yogurt, ½ cup
sour cream, 1 TBS
coriander leaves (cilantro),
    1 tsp
garlic, 1 clove*

Other Ingredients
*vegetable oil, ½-1 TBS
salt, ½ tsp and a pinch
sugar, ½ tsp
peanuts, roasted, 1 TBS*

Spices
*hing, 2 pinches
seeds mixture, ½ tsp
turmeric, ¼ tsp
hot red pepper powder, ⅛ tsp
    and a pinch
cumin/coriander powder
    ¼ tsp*

Mix together and set aside:
>**½ cup yogurt**
>**½ cup water**
>**1 Tablespoon sour cream**
>**1 Tablespoon Peanut Chutney (pg. 45, or see below)**
>**½ teaspoon salt**

In a small saucepan, heat until the seeds pop:
>**½-1 Tablespoon vegetable oil**
>**pinch hing**
>**1 teaspoon fresh coriander leaves (cilantro),**
>**   chopped**
>**½ teaspoon cumin/mustard/sesame seed mixture**
>**¼ teaspoon turmeric**
>**⅛ teaspoon hot red pepper powder**
>**1 clove garlic, minced**

Pour the hot spice mixture into the yogurt mixture, and add:
>**½ teaspoon sugar**
>**more water as needed to make consistency**
>**   either like heavy cream or a thin paste**

Stir well, breaking up any lumps to make a smooth consistency. This chutney goes very well with *Tomato Pancakes*, pg. 80, or with *Sweet Filled Paratha*, pg. 77.

PEANUT CHUTNEY (Below is for amount needed in this recipe. For a larger quantity, see *Peanut Chutney*, pg. 45.)

Grind together into a fine powder:
>**1 Tablespoon roasted peanuts**
>**¼ teaspoon cumin/coriander powder**
>**pinch hot red pepper powder**
>**pinch salt**
>**pinch hing**

ZUCCHINI SPINE CHUTNEY

INTERESTING CHUTNEY MADE FROM THE SPINES OF INDIAN ZUCCHINIS

Indian zucchinis have long, thin ridges under the surface of the peel. Though called "spines," these ridges are not sharp. You can easily peel them off the zucchini with a vegetable peeler.

In a small frying pan, heat:
> **1 Tablespoon vegetable oil**

Add and sauté till browned:
> **¾-1 cup Indian zucchini spines, chopped**
> **2 Tablespoons fresh hot green pepper, chopped**
> **1 Tablespoon fresh coriander leaves (cilantro), chopped**
> **1 teaspoon salt**
> **½ teaspoon cumin seeds**
> **¼ teaspoon sesame seeds**
> **1 dried hot pepper (opt.)**

Grind the above mixture into a coarse paste in a blender.

In the same frying pan, heat:
> **¼ teaspoon vegetable oil**
> **pinch hing**
> **¼ teaspoon cumin/mustard/sesame seed mixture**

When the seeds pop, remove the pan from the heat, add the contents of the blender, and mix well.

Don't be put off by this chutney's unusual appearance; it tastes delicious!

Makes about 1 cup
(traditional serving = 1-2 tsp)

Per serving: Calories: 5, Protein: 0 gm., Fat: 0.5 gm., Carbohydrates: 0 gm.

• • • •

Fresh Ingredients
spines from Indian zucchini, 1 cup
hot green pepper, 2 TBS
coriander leaves (cilantro), 1 TBS

Other Ingredients
vegetable oil, 1 TBS + ¼ tsp
salt, 1 tsp
sesame seeds, ¼ tsp

Spices
cumin seeds, ½ tsp
(optional: dried hot pepper, 1)
hing, pinch
seeds mixture, ¼ tsp

SALADS & PICKLES

BEET SALAD
GRATED BEETS, LIGHTLY SEASONED

Makes 1 cup
(traditional serving = 2 TBS)

Per serving: Calories: 5,
Protein: 0 gm., Fat: 0 gm.,
Carbohydrates: 1 gm

• • • •

Fresh Ingredients
beet, 1 large or 2 medium
lime juice, 1 tsp

Other Ingredients
sugar, ½ tsp
salt, ½ -1 tsp

Spices
black pepper, ground,
  ½ -1 tsp
cumin/coriander powder,
  ¼ tsp

In a small saucepan, boil in water for 5 minutes:
1 large or 2 medium beets, peeled

It will still be quite firm. Then grate or shred it.

In a small bowl, combine the shredded beet with:
½ teaspoon sugar
½-1 teaspoon salt (to taste)
½-1 teaspoon ground black pepper (to taste)
¼ teaspoon cumin/coriander powder
1 teaspoon lime juice

CABBAGE SALAD
GRATED CABBAGE, LIGHTLY SEASONED

In a bowl, mix:
> **1 cup raw cabbage, shredded**
> **½ Tablespoon fresh coriander leaves (cilantro), chopped**
> **1 teaspoon vegetable oil**
> **pinch salt**
> **pinch hing**
> **pinch garam masala**
> **hot red pepper powder to taste**

For a spicier cabbage salad, mix in an additional:
> **1 teaspoon vegetable oil**
> **more hot red pepper powder to taste**
> **pinch salt**
> **pinch cumin/coriander powder**
> **pinch cumin seeds**
> **pinch garam masala**

As a variation to either salad, you may add:
> **fresh tomato, chopped (opt.)**

Makes 1 cup
(traditional serving = 2 TBS)

Per serving: Calories: 12, Protein: 0 gm., Fat: 1.1 gm., Carbohydrates: 0 gm.

• • • •

Fresh Ingredients
cabbage, 1 cup raw
coriander leaves (cilantro), ½ TBS
(optional: tomato to taste)

Other Ingredients
salt, pinch
vegetable oil, 1-2 tsp

Spices
hing, pinch
garam masala, pinch
hot red pepper powder, to taste
(optional: cumin/coriander powder, pinch)
(optional: cumin seeds, ¼ tsp)
(optional: garam masala, additional pinch)

CARROT SALAD
SEASONED, SHREDDED CARROTS
FLAVORED WITH CRUSHED PEANUTS

Makes 1½ cups
(traditional serving = 2 TBS)

Per serving: Calories: 21,
Protein: 0 gm., Fat: 1.4 gm.,
Carbohydrates: 1 gm.

• • • •

Fresh Ingredients
carrots, 2
coriander leaves (cilantro),
  2 TBS
(optional: lemon or lime
  juice, 1 tsp)

Other Ingredients
peanuts, roasted, 1 TBS
salt, 1 tsp
sugar, 1 tsp
vegetable oil, 1 TBS

Spices
hing, pinch
seeds mixture, 1 tsp
cumin/coriander powder,
  ½ tsp
hot red pepper powder, ½ tsp

In a blender, mortar and pestle, or bag with a rolling pin, crush:
> **1 Tablespoon roasted peanuts**

Mix crushed peanuts in a bowl with:
> **2 carrots, shredded**
> **1 teaspoon salt**
> **1 teaspoon sugar**

Heat in a small saucepan until the seeds pop, then remove from the heat:
> **1 Tablespoon vegetable oil**
> **pinch hing**
> **1 teaspoon cumin/mustard/sesame seeds mixture**

Add to the saucepan mixture:
> **½ teaspoon cumin/coriander powder**
> **½ teaspoon hot red pepper powder**
> **2 Tablespoons fresh coriander leaves (cilantro), chopped**
> **1 teaspoon lemon or lime juice (opt.)**

Combine the carrots and the marinade, mix well, and chill.

CARROT SALAD WITH DAL
SHREDDED CARROT SALAD WITH MUNG BEANS

In a small bowl, soak for 1 hour in 2 cups water, then drain:
    ¼ cup green mung beans

In a medium-sized bowl, combine the beans with:
    3 carrots, shredded (about 1 cup)
    ½ fresh jalapeño pepper, diced
    1 Tablespoon fresh coriander leaves (cilantro),
        chopped
    1 Tablespoon lemon juice, or more to taste
    1½ teaspoons roasted peanuts, crushed
    1 teaspoon salt
    ½ teaspoon sugar
    ¼ teaspoon cumin/coriander powder

Makes 1½ cups
(traditional serving = 2 TBS)

*Per serving: Calories: 18,
Protein: 1 gm., Fat: 0.3 gm.,
Carbohydrates: 3 gm.*

• • • •

Fresh Ingredients
*carrots, 3
jalapeño pepper, ½
coriander leaves (cilantro),
    1 TBS
lemon juice, 1 TBS*

Other Ingredients
*green mung beans, ¼ cup
peanuts, roasted, 1½ tsp
salt, 1 tsp
sugar, ½ tsp*

Spices
*cumin/coriander powder,
    ¼ tsp*

CUCUMBER RAITA

SEASONED SALAD OF YOGURT AND CUCUMBER

Makes about 2 cups
(traditional serving = 3 TBS)

Per serving: Calories: 20,
Protein: 1 gm., Fat: 0.8 gm.,
Carbohydrates: 2 gm.

• • • •

Fresh Ingredients
yogurt, 1 cup
cucumber, 1
(optional: tomato, ½)
milk, 2 TBS
onion, raw, 1 TBS
coriander leaves (cilantro),
*   2 TBS*
(optional: sour cream,
*   1 TBS)*

Other Ingredients
salt ½ tsp

Spices
cumin seeds, 1 TBS
hot red pepper powder,
*   2 pinches*

Roast in a dry skillet, stirring constantly, until lightly browned (about 2-3 minutes):
   1 Tablespoon cumin seeds

Grind seeds in a blender or mortar and pestle.

Combine the ground seeds in a bowl with:
   1 cup yogurt
   1 cucumber, peeled and shredded
   ½ medium tomato, chopped small (opt.)
   2 Tablespoons milk
   2 Tablespoons fresh coriander leaves (cilantro),
      chopped
   1 Tablespoon onion, chopped
   1 Tablespoon sour cream (opt.)
   ½ teaspoon salt
   2 pinches hot red pepper powder
   1-2 Tablespoons water, enough to make a creamy
      consistency

Serve in individual small bowls or cups.

LIME PICKLE
SWEET AND SPICY STEAMED LIMES

Chop into ⅛ths:
  2 limes

Place in a steamer, cover, and steam for 10 minutes, until soft.

Add:
  1 Tablespoon sugar
  ½ teaspoon salt
  ¼ teaspoon turmeric
  ¼ teaspoon hot red pepper powder, or to taste

Mix well.

Makes about 1 cup
(traditional serving = 2 TBS)

*Per serving: Calories: 11,
Protein: 0 gm., Fat: 0 gm.,
Carbohydrates: 2 gm.*

• • • •

Fresh Ingredients
limes, 2

Other Ingredients
sugar, 1 TBS
salt, ½ tsp

Spices
turmeric, ¼ tsp
hot red pepper powder, ¼ tsp
 or to taste

RADISH PICKLE

HOT AND SPICY, SEASONED SLICED RADISHES

Makes ¾ cup
(traditional serving = 1-2 TBS)

Per serving: Calories: 12,
Protein: 0 gm., Fat: 0.8 gm.,
Carbohydrates: 1 gm.

• • • •

Fresh Ingredients
lime juice, 1 TBS
radishes, any kind, ½ cup
coriander leaves (cilantro),
* 1½ tsp*
(optional: carrots, ½ cup)

Other Ingredients
vegetable oil, 1½ tsp
sugar, 1½ tsp
salt, 1 tsp

Spices
mustard seeds, 1½ tsp
hing, pinch
seeds mixture, ½ tsp
turmeric, ¼ tsp
cumin/coriander powder,
* ¼ tsp*
hot red pepper powder, ¼ tsp
* or to taste*

Crush into powder in a plastic bag with a rolling pin, and set aside:
> **1½ teaspoons mustard seeds**

Heat in a small saucepan until the seeds pop, then remove from the heat:
> **1½ teaspoons vegetable oil**
> **pinch hing**
> **½ teaspoon cumin/mustard/sesame seeds mixture**

Add and mix well:
> **¼ teaspoon turmeric**
> **¼ teaspoon cumin/coriander powder**
> **¼ teaspoon hot red pepper powder, or to taste**
> **all the crushed mustard seeds**

Add:
> **1 Tablespoon lime juice (juice from ¼ lime)**
> **1½ teaspoons fresh coriander leaves (cilantro), chopped**
> **1½ teaspoons white sugar**
> **1 teaspoon salt**

Then add:
> **½ cup radishes (any kind), thinly sliced**

If you wish, you may double the spices and add:
> **½ cup carrots, thinly sliced (opt.)**

Mix well and chill.

SPINACH RAITA
SEASONED SALAD WITH YOGURT AND SPINACH

In a small, dry skillet, stirring constantly, roast until lightly browned (about 2-3 minutes):

> ½ teaspoon cumin seeds

Grind the seeds in a blender or mortar and pestle.

In a bowl, combine:

> ½ cup yogurt
> 1½ Tablespoons milk
> 1½ Tablespoons water
> 1½ teaspoons sour cream
> the roasted, ground cumin seeds
> ¼ teaspoon salt
> pinch hot red pepper powder, or to taste
> pinch cumin/coriander powder
> 1 cup fresh or ¾ cup frozen spinach, finely chopped
> 1 small carrot, diced or grated
> 1½ red radishes, diced or grated
> 1½ teaspoons fresh coriander leaves (cilantro), chopped
> 1½ teaspoons fresh raw onion, diced
> ½ small tomato, diced
> ½ scallion, diced

Add enough water so that the dressing for the salad is the consistency of heavy cream. You may garnish this salad with hot pepper powder, cumin/coriander powder, and sliced fresh scallion.

Makes 1½ cups
(traditional serving = 3 TBS)

Per serving: Calories: 19, Protein: 1 gm., Fat: 0.7 gm., Carbohydrates: 2 gm.

• • • •

Fresh Ingredients
yogurt, plain, ½ cup
milk, 1½ TBS
sour cream, 1½ tsp
spinach, 1 cup fresh
*   (or ¾ cup frozen)*
carrot, 1 small
red radishes, 1½
coriander leaves (cilantro),
*   1½ tsp*
onion, 1½ tsp
tomato, ½ small
scallion, ½

Other Ingredients
salt, ¼ tsp

Spices
cumin seeds, ½ tsp
hot red pepper powder, pinch
*   or to taste*
cumin/coriander powder,
*   pinch*

BREADS

ဢ   ဢ   ဢ

ALOO PARATHA
POTATO-FILLED FLAT BREAD

Makes 9
(traditional serving = 1)

*Per serving: Calories: 143,
Protein: 4 gm., Fat: 1.6 gm.,
Carbohydrates: 13 gm.*

••••

Fresh Ingredients
*potatoes, 3 large
onion, ¾ cup
coriander leaves (cilantro),
   3 TBS*

Other Ingredients
*Indian whole wheat flour,
   2¼ cups
salt, 2 tsp
vegetable oil for sautéing*

Spices
*cumin/coriander powder,
   1½ TBS
garam masala, ¾ tsp
hot red pepper powder,
   ¼ tsp or to taste*

To make a dough, mix in a shallow, flat bowl or pan:
> **2¼ cups Indian whole wheat flour**
> **½ teaspoon salt**

Add:
> **about ¾ cup warm water (enough to make a
> bread-like dough)**

Cover and set aside.
To make the stuffing, boil, peel, and mash:
> **3 large potatoes (about 3 cups)**

Add:
> **¾ cup onion, finely chopped**
> **3 Tablespoons fresh coriander leaves (cilantro),
>   finely chopped**
> **1½ Tablespoons cumin/coriander powder**
> **1½ teaspoon salt**
> **¾ teaspoon garam masala**
> **¼ teaspoon hot red pepper powder, or to taste**

Method I: To form the paratha, make 18 equal-sized balls of
dough. Using all-purpose white flour as needed, roll out 2 of
the balls into 5" rounds until about ¼ inch thick. Place about
2-3 Tablespoons of the filling on one round, and cover with
the other. Press gently around the edges, then careful roll
out the paratha until about ¼" thick and 6½" wide all
together.

Method II: You can also form the paratha by dividing the
dough into 9 equal parts. Roll out each part until about 10"
wide and ¼" thick. Place about ¼ cup of the filling in the
center, and gather the dough circle up around the filling,
drawing the dough up to a sealed point at the top. Fold over
the point and flatten the dough into a thick patty. Roll out
carefully until about ¼ inch thick and 6½" wide.

To sauté the paratha, preheat a frying pan on medium high heat. Add 1 teaspoon oil for the first paratha only. Put in one paratha and paint the top surface with about ¼ teaspoon oil. Flip and paint second side. Continue to flip the paratha frequently, pressing with a spatula on any unbrowned areas until browned all over on both sides. Remove from the pan and repeat with the other parathas until all are cooked. Serve topped with ghee or plain yogurt.

CHAPATI
WHOLE WHEAT FLAT BREADS

Mix together:
>   2 cups Indian whole wheat flour
>   1 teaspoon salt
>   1 Tablespoon vegetable oil
>   about ¾ cup warm water (enough for a
>   kneadable dough)

Makes 10-12
(traditional serving = 1)

*Per serving: Calories: 92,
Protein: 3 gm., Fat: 1.6 gm.,
Carbohydrates: 16 gm.*

• • • •

Fresh Ingredients

Other Ingredients
*Indian whole wheat flour,
    2 cups
salt, 1 tsp
vegetable oil, 1 TBS
ghee, about ¼ cup*

Spices

Knead the dough, cover, and leave aside for at least ½ hour or, ideally, up to 2 hours. After about 1 hour (or right before rolling out), punch the dough and knead again without any more water.

Make 10-12 1½" balls; dip each one into dry whole wheat flour, and roll out into thin, 6" circles. Place a flat, ungreased griddle on the stove at medium high heat. When hot, place a rolled-out chapati "right side" down on the griddle. (The "right side" is the one facing you when you roll it.) When bubbles are visible, turn over and cook until tiny brown spots appear on the side facing the griddle.

If you have a gas stove, hold the chapati with a pair of tongs, and place it directly over the burner flame for a few seconds, until the chapati puffs up. Turn and repeat on the other side.

If you have an electric stove, keep the chapati on the griddle. With a wadded-up paper towel to protect your fingers, press *gently* all around the chapati. Flip the chapati and press gently around the other side. This procedure should make the chapati puff up. (If you press too hard, the chapati will become too crunchy.)

Remove the chapati from the heat, and butter with ghee on the "right side."

(cont.)

Some of the foods that are traditionally served with chapatis are *Lentils with Scallions*, pg. 108, *Spicy Mung Beans*, pg. 111, eggplant dishes, green bean dishes, spinach dishes, and zucchini dishes.

BROWN SUGAR CHAPATI
CHAPATI MADE WITH BROWN SUGAR

In a bowl place:
> ½ cup warm milk (or water)

Slowly add:
> ¼ cup brown sugar (Indian if possible)

In a separate bowl, mix:
> 1½ cups Indian whole wheat flour
> 1 Tablespoon vegetable oil

Mix the milk and sugar into the flour mixture, and knead. The dough will be dry. Roll out into a long tube, and pinch off 12 walnut-sized balls. Press each ball and dip into oil. Roll out into 5" circles on an oiled board. Sprinkle oil on a hot frying pan. Flip the chapati onto the pan, and let bubble; then turn over. Sprinkle the first side with oil while the second side cooks briefly. Turn and cook the first side again while pressing the edges with a paper towel to make the chapati puff up. Sprinkle the second side (facing you) with oil. Turn again and press the edges while frying the second side. Each side cooks twice, the second time with sprinkled oil.

Serve with *Peanut Chutney*, pg. 45. These keep very well and are great to nibble while traveling.

Makes 12
(traditional serving = 1)

Per serving: Calories: 78, Protein: 2 gm., Fat: 1.6 gm., Carbohydrates: 13 gm.

• • • •

Fresh Ingredients
milk, ½ cup

Other Ingredients
brown sugar, Indian if possible, ¼ cup
Indian whole wheat flour, 1½ cups
vegetable oil, about 2 TBS

Spices

Makes about 14
(traditional serving = 1)

*Per serving: Calories: 105,
Protein: 2 gm., Fat: 3.9 gm.,
Carbohydrates: 15 gm.*

• • • •

Fresh Ingredients
*corn, 2 mature ears
coriander leaves (cilantro),
1 TBS
jalapeño pepper, 1
lemon juice, 1 TBS*

Other Ingredients
*Indian whole wheat flour,
2 cups
butter, 1 TBS
salt, 2 tsp
vegetable oil, 3 TBS and for
deep frying*

Spices
*cumin seeds, 1 tsp
hing, pinch
seeds mixture, ½ tsp
cumin/coriander powder
½ tsp
turmeric, ¼ tsp*

CORN KACHURI
Fried Flat Breads Filled with Seasoned Corn

In a bowl, combine and knead together:
> **2 cups Indian whole wheat flour**
> **1 Tablespoon butter**
> **1 Tablespoon vegetable oil**
> **1 teaspoon salt**
> **about ¾ cup warm water (enough for a firm
> dough)**

Cover and let rest. Meanwhile, grind together coarsely in a blender or food processor:
> **raw kernels from 2 ears of mature corn* (about
> 1½ cups)**
> **1 Tablespoon fresh coriander leaves (cilantro),
> chopped**
> **1 fresh jalapeño pepper, chopped**
> **1 teaspoon salt**
> **1 teaspoon cumin seeds**

In a saucepan, heat:
> **2 Tablespoons oil**
> **pinch hing**
> **½ teaspoon cumin/mustard/sesame seed mixture**

When the seeds pop, add:
> **1 Tablespoon lemon juice**
> **¼-½ teaspoon cumin/coriander powder**
> **¼ teaspoon turmeric**

Add the corn mixture, and cook over low heat, uncovered, for 10-15 minutes until dry-ish and lightly browned. Break off 1" pieces of dough, and roll out on an oiled board into 3" rounds. Put 1-2 teaspoons of the corn mixture between two of the rounds, and roll slightly to join the two rounds. Deep-fry in oil until golden brown, like puris.

*young, cooked, or frozen corn is also OK

CORN CHAPATI
CORNMEAL FLAT BREADS (SIMILAR TO CORN TORTILLAS)

Mix together with a spoon:
> **2 cups white masa harina***
> **1 teaspoon salt**
> **½ cup boiling water**

Add more warm water as needed for a soft dough, about ½-1 cup.

Knead with wet hands. Divide into 8 roughly equal portions. Pat out each piece into a thin round on a surface floured with more masa harina. Place the chapati, one at a time, on a heated, ungreased griddle. Moisten the top surface of the chapati with a wet paper towel. Flip it when the bottom side is slightly browned. When the second side is slightly browned, briefly place the chapati directly over the flame, browning both sides.

*It is important that the masa harina be *very* finely ground.

Makes 8
(traditional serving = 1)

Per serving: Calories: 125, Protein: 3 gm., Fat: 0 gm., Carbohydrates: 27 gm.

• • • •

Fresh Ingredients

Other Ingredients
white masa harina, 2 cups
salt, 1 tsp
flour for rolling out

Spices

DOSA
SOUR PANCAKES

Makes nine 6" pancakes
(traditional serving = 1)

*Per serving: Calories: 102,
Protein: 2 gm., Fat: 0 gm.,
Carbohydrates: 22 gm.*

• • • •

Fresh Ingredients

Other Ingredients
*rice flour, 1½ cups
urad dal flour,* ½ cup
salt, ½ tsp
vegetable oil for sautéing
ghee, for spreading*

Spices
fenugreek, ¼ tsp

Mix in a bowl and soak for ½ -1½ days (the longer you soak, the more sour the mixture becomes):
> **1½ cups rice flour**
> **½ cup urad dal flour***
> **½ teaspoon salt**
> **¼ teaspoon fenugreek**
> **enough water to make a semi-thin paste (about 2¼ cups)**

When you are ready to fry the dosa, heat a small amount of oil in a skillet. Add a ¼-cup scoopful of batter, and smear it with the scoop to make a thin, flat "pancake." Add a small amount of oil at the edges and on the top side of the pancake. When browned, flip and brown the second side. Spread ghee on the first side (now facing up). When the second side is browned, fold the dosa in half, and remove from heat.

The batter will keep well in the refrigerator.

Dosa can be eaten filled with potato curry. For a nice variation, make the batter thicker, and spoon the onion and spice mixture from the recipe for *Idli Pancakes*, pg. 69, over the batter before you turn it on the griddle.

*If you don't have urad dal flour, you can soak ¼ cup green mung beans overnight. Puree in a blender with about 6 Tablespoons water. Use this puree instead of the flour, decreasing the water you use to make the semi-thin paste.

IDLI PANCAKES
Seasoned Pancakes

Mix together:
> 1 onion, finely chopped
> 1 Tablespoon fresh coriander leaves (cilantro),
> chopped
> 1 teaspoon cumin/coriander powder
> 1 teaspoon salt
> ½ teaspoon cumin seeds
> pinch hot pepper powder
> pinch chopped fresh hot pepper/ginger/garlic
> mixture*
> 1 tomato, finely chopped (opt.)

Following the package directions, add about 1⅓-1½ cups water to make a thin batter to:
> 1 (200 gm) package idli mix (uthupa)

Spoon about ¼ cup batter onto a hot, oiled griddle. Sprinkle with the onion mixture and a drizzle of oil. Brown and flip. Brown on the other side, and serve. This can be eaten with *Dosa Chutney*, pg. 39.

Traditionally, idli are steamed wheat cakes, requiring a special steamer to cook them. This recipe gives you an opportunity to enjoy their flavor without having to purchase additional equipment. You can also use idli mix, made a little thicker, for dumplings for plain lentil soup.

*See recipe for *Chana*, pg. 104.

Makes 8
(traditional serving = 1)

Per serving: Calories: 61, Protein: 2 gm., Fat: 0.8 gm., Carbohydrates: 11 gm.

••••

Fresh Ingredients
onion, 1
coriander leaves (cilantro),
* 1 TBS*
hot green pepper, pinch
ginger pinch
garlic, pinch
(optional: tomato, 1)

Other Ingredients
salt, 1 tsp
idli mix, 1 package
vegetable oil for sautéing

Spices
cumin/coriander powder,
* 1 tsp*
cumin seeds, ½ tsp
hot red pepper powder, pinch

MOULI PARATHA
Whole Wheat Flat Breads Filled with Seasoned, Grated Radish

Makes 8 paratha
(traditional serving = 1)

*Per serving: Calories: 123,
Protein: 4 gm., Fat: 2 gm.,
Carbohydrates: 22 gm.*

• • • •

Fresh Ingredients
*daikon radish, 1 cup
coriander leaves (cilantro),
1 TBS*

Other Ingredients
*salt, 1½ tsp
Indian whole wheat flour,
2 cups
vegetable oil, 1 TBS + for
sautéing*

Spices
*cumin/coriander powder,
1 tsp
hot red pepper powder, 1 tsp
garam masala, ½ tsp*

In a bowl, combine by hand:

> 1 cup fresh grated daikon radish (squeeze the moisture out)
> 1 Tablespoon fresh coriander leaves (cilantro), chopped
> 1 teaspoon cumin/coriander powder
> 1 teaspoon hot red pepper powder
> ½ teaspoon garam masala
> ½ teaspoon salt

Prepare a dough by mixing together:

> 2 cups Indian whole wheat flour
> 1 teaspoon salt
> 1 Tablespoon vegetable oil
> about ¾ cup warm water (enough for a kneadable dough)

Using one of the following two methods, prepare the paratha:

Method I: Divide the dough into 16 pieces. Roll out 2 pieces into 4½" disks. Layer 1-2 Tablespoons of the radish mixture between the two rounds, and carefully roll out to 6" in diameter. Repeat for the remaining pieces.

Method II: Divide the dough into 8 pieces. Roll out each piece into a 6" disk. Place 1-2 Tablespoons of the radish mixture in the center of each disk, draw up the edges to the center and pinch; then carefully roll out to 6" in diameter again.

Place each paratha on a dry griddle, and brown both sides. Then paint each side with a small amount of oil (or ghee), and briefly brown again on both sides.

PURI
FRIED, PUFFED WHOLE WHEAT FLAT BREADS

Mix together in a bowl:
> **2 cups Indian whole wheat flour**
> **½ Tablespoon vegetable oil**
> **salt to taste**

Slowly add about ¾ cup warm water, just enough to form a firm dough, and knead till smooth. Cover, let rest at least ½ hour, and knead again briefly. If resting more than 1 hour, punch and knead dough again before rolling out.

Divide into small balls about golf-ball size, and roll out into 6" rounds on an oiled board. Heat vegetable oil in a wok or saucepan. Add a little salt to the oil to keep it from smoking. Fry the puri one at a time, holding them under the oil on the first side until they puff. Turn and fry till light brown; drain.

Serve as soon as possible; these breads are not as good later.

Puri are traditionally served with any or all of the following: *Chana* (chickpeas), pg. 104, *Black-eyed Pea Curry*, pg. 102, *Spinach Dal*, pg. 112, *Potato Curry*, pg. 141, *Brussels Sprouts*, pg. 121, and anything with yogurt in it.

For spicy puris:
When making the dough, add to the dry ingredients pinches of:
> **turmeric**
> **hot pepper**
> **cumin/coriander powder**
> **hing**

Makes 10-12
(traditional serving = 1)

Per serving: Calories: 86, Protein: 3 gm., Fat: 1 gm., Carbohydrates: 16 gm.

• • • •

Fresh Ingredients

Other Ingredients
Indian whole wheat flour, 2 cups
vegetable oil, ½ TBS and for deep frying
salt, to taste

Spices

SELF-RISING PURI
FRIED, LEAVENED, WHITE FLOUR FLAT BREADS

Makes 10
(traditional serving = 1)

*Per serving: Calories: 103,
Protein: 3 gm., Fat: 0.9 gm.,
Carbohydrates: 20 gm.*

• • • •

Fresh Ingredients
milk, 1 cup

Other Ingredients
*self-rising white flour,
    2 cups and for kneading
vegetable oil for deep frying*

Spices

In a flat-bottomed bowl, mix together into a sticky dough:
**2 cups self-rising white flour
about 1 cup lukewarm milk**

Knead until smooth, though still sticky. Let rest, loosely covered, for 15-20 minutes.

Break off golf ball-sized pieces, dip in the self-rising flour, and roll out as for puri. Deep-fry in oil until very lightly browned, pressing down lightly into the oil to assist puffing. Turn once to brown the second side lightly. Remove from the oil, drain, and serve.

These do not keep well, so eat immediately. These puri are especially good with *Chana*, pg. 104.

SAMOSA
FRIED, POTATO-FILLED DOUGH POCKETS

To make the samosa filling, heat in a skillet:
>**1 Tablespoon vegetable oil**
>**pinch hing**
>**½ teaspoon cumin/mustard/sesame seed mixture**

When the seeds pop, add:
>**1 medium onion, finely chopped**
>**1 Tablespoon fresh coriander leaves (cilantro), chopped**

Sauté until the onion becomes translucent, then add:
>**½ Tablespoon amchur (mango) powder, or 1 Tablespoon lemon juice**
>**1 teaspoon cumin/coriander powder**
>**½ teaspoon salt**
>**pinch hot red pepper powder**

Sauté a few minutes, then add:
>**3 medium potatoes, boiled, peeled, and cut into very small pieces**
>**¼ cup frozen peas (opt.)**

Mix well and sauté just until heated through, then remove from heat and set aside.

To make the samosa dough, mix in a bowl:
>**2 cups white flour**
>**2½ Tablespoons vegetable oil**
>**1½ Tablespoons rice flour**
>**½ teaspoon salt**

Add water gradually (about ¼ cup) until the dough holds together, and knead well. Roll into a ball and cover with a moist cloth. Let rest about 20 minutes.

(cont.)

Makes 30

Per serving: Calories: 56, Protein: 1 gm., Fat: 0.9 gm., Carbohydrates: 9 gm.

• • • •

Fresh Ingredients
*onion, 1 medium
coriander leaves (cilantro),
 1 TBS
potato, 3 medium
(optional: peas, ¼ cup)*

Other Ingredients
*vegetable oil, 3½ TBS and
 for deep frying
salt, 1 tsp
white flour, 2 cups
rice four, 1½ TBS*

Spices
*hing, pinch
seeds mixture, ½ tsp
amchur (mango) powder,
 ½ TBS
cumin/coriander powder,
 1 tsp
hot red pepper powder, pinch*

To assemble the samosas, break off 1½"-2" pieces of dough, and roll out into 6"-8" diameter circles. Cut each circle in half. Fold each half-circle in thirds to make a pie-wedge shape. Seal the point by pressing or pinching. Pick up the dough, and seal the outside edge by pinching to form a cone. Fill the cone two-thirds with potato mixture. Moisten the lip of the cone with a little milk or water, and pinch to seal. Press the samosa between your palms to remove air pockets. Flute the top edge and cover with a moist cloth until ready to fry.

To cook the samosa, deep fry until browned, turning twice; drain. Serve with *Tamarind-Date Chutney*, pg. 46.

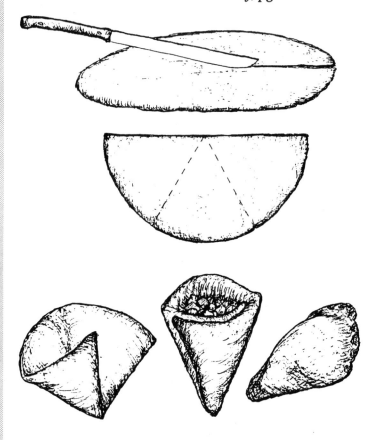

SPICY BESAN ROTI

SPICY WHOLE WHEAT AND CHICKPEA ROUNDS

Mix together:

>1 cup Indian whole wheat flour
>1 cup chickpea flour
>2 small onions, diced
>2 Tablespoons fresh coriander leaves (cilantro), chopped
>1½ to 2 teaspoons cumin/coriander powder
>1 teaspoon salt
>½-¾ teaspoon hot pepper powder
>½ teaspoon turmeric
>½ teaspoon fresh hot green pepper, minced
>¼ teaspoon ginger, grated
>⅛ teaspoon garlic, minced
>pinch hing
>pinch cumin seeds

Add enough water to form a sticky dough—about 1 cup. Knead well.

Wet a piece of paper towel, and fold into a square. Form a 2" ball in your wet palm, place on the wet paper towel, and press into a 4" circle with wet fingers. Make 5 holes in the circle with a wet finger. Place on a hot, lightly oiled skillet by laying the flattened round on the skillet with the paper towel facing up, then peeling off the paper towel. Drizzle oil into the holes and around the circumference. Brown and flip. Brown the other side and drain on a fresh paper towel. Moisten the wet paper towel, and begin the next round.

As you get more adept at making these, just fold the paper towel in half, and make two rounds on the towel at a time, taking them to the griddle, flipping both over, and peeling back the towel.

Eat with butter, sugar, yogurt, vegetables, or some combination of these.

Makes 8
(traditional serving = 1)

Per serving: Calories: 97, Protein: 4 gm., Fat: 0.8 gm., Carbohydrates: 18 gm.

• • • •

Fresh Ingredients
onions, 2 small
coriander leaves (cilantro), 2 TBS
hot green pepper, ½ tsp
ginger, ¼ tsp
garlic, ⅛ tsp

Other Ingredients
Indian whole wheat flour, 1 cup
chickpea flour, 1 cup
salt, 1 tsp
vegetable oil for sautéing

Spices
cumin/coriander powder, 1½ tsp
hot red pepper powder, ½-¾ tsp
turmeric, ½ tsp
hing, pinch
cumin seeds, pinch

SWEET CHAPATI
WHOLE WHEAT FLAT BREADS WITH SUGAR FILLING

Makes 9
(traditional serving = 1)

*Per serving: Calories: 153,
Protein: 5 gm., Fat: 2.7 gm.,
Carbohydrates: 27 gm.*

• • • •

Fresh Ingredients

Other Ingredients
*Indian whole wheat flour,
   3 cups and for kneading
salt, 1½ tsp
vegetable oil, 1½ TBS
sugar, crystallized, for
   sprinkling
ghee for sautéing*

Spices

Mix together:
> **3 cups Indian whole wheat flour**
> **1½ teaspoons salt**
> **1½ Tablespoon vegetable oil**
> **about 1-1¼ cups warm water (enough for a
>   kneadable dough)**

Knead the dough and leave aside for at least ½ hour (ideally for 1-2 hours). After about 1 hour (or right before rolling out), punch the dough and knead again without any more water.

Make 18 walnut- to lemon-sized balls, dip each one into dry whole wheat flour, and roll out very thin.

Sprinkle one uncooked chapati with:
> **sugar (crystallized is best)**

Cover the sugared chapati with a plain, uncooked chapati, sandwich-style. Press around the edges with your fingers, and roll out the pair a little more to bond the two pieces.

Place a flat, ungreased griddle on the stove at medium high heat. When hot, place a rolled-out double chapati on the griddle. Paint the top with ghee. When the under-side is browned, flip and paint again with ghee. When second side is browned, flip again to each side briefly. Remove from the pan and begin the next double chapati.

This bread is a favorite with children. A similar treat can be made using regular chapati. Make chapati according to the recipe on page 64, then spread with ghee and sugar, roll up, and eat.

SWEET FILLED PARATHA
Whole Wheat Flat Bread Filled With Sweet Bean Paste

To make the dough, combine in a medium-sized bowl:
> **3 cups sifted Indian whole wheat flour (must be very fine)**
> **½ teaspoon salt**
> **2 Tablespoons vegetable oil**
> **1 cup warm water**

Knead well, cover, and let rest.

To make the filling, combine in a saucepan:
> **2 cups raw split yellow peas**
> **4 cups water (enough to cover)**

Simmer about 30–45 minutes until soft, adding more water as needed to keep the peas from sticking to the pan. Drain off the water and save it and a teaspoon of cooked peas for *Sweet Paratha Sauce*, pg. 81.

Puree the peas, setting aside about ¼-⅓ cup of puree for the sauce as well as the cooked whole peas and cooking water, then add to the puree for the paratha:
> **1¾ cups white sugar**

Cook the sweetened puree for 15 to 20 minutes in the microwave, stirring every 5 minutes, or cook for about 45 minutes on the stove over low heat, stirring frequently.

When thickened, add:
> **1 Tablespoon cardamom powder, or less to taste**
> **½ teaspoon ginger powder**

(cont.)

Makes 10
(traditional serving = 1)

Per serving: Calories: 363, Protein: 10 gm., Fat: 3.2 gm., Carbohydrates: 73 gm.

• • • •

Fresh Ingredients

Other Ingredients
Indian whole wheat flour, 3 cups
vegetable oil, 2 TBS
salt, ½ tsp
yellow split peas, 2 cups raw
sugar, 1¾ cups
ghee, for sautéing

Spices
cardamom powder, 1 TBS
ginger powder, ½ tsp

Make sure the filling is thick or it will squish out the sides when the paratha are rolled. This filling can keep for several days in the refrigerator.

To fill the dough, use either one of the following two methods:

Method 1: Divide the dough into 20 equal pieces. Roll these into balls and cover. Take out 2 balls at a time, and roll them on a floured surface into 5" rounds. Place about 2 Tablespoons of filling on one round. Cover with the second round, and press the edges to seal. Gently roll out to about 6½" wide.

Method II: Divide the dough in 10 equal pieces, roll into balls of dough, and cover. Roll out on a floured surface to 5" wide. Wrap each circle of dough around 2 Tablespoons of filling shaped in a ball, and seal the seams in the dough. Gently roll out again to 6½" wide; try not to pick up the circle while rolling out.

To cook the paratha, heat a frying pan on medium-low heat with a little bit of ghee. Gently place a paratha in the pan, and lightly brown both sides. Now, paint the side facing up with ghee, press, and flip; paint the second side and press again. Fold in half and briefly flip both sides one more time. Remove from the pan onto a dish lined with a paper towel.

These are very sweet and filling, and taste best dipped in *Sweet Paratha Sauce, pg. 81.*

TANDOORI ROTI
BAKED WHOLE WHEAT FLAT BREADS

Preheat oven to 350°.

Mix together:

> **2 cups Indian whole wheat flour**
> **1 teaspoon salt**
> **1 Tablespoon vegetable oil**
> **about ¾ cup warm water (enough for a kneadable dough)**

Knead the dough, cover, and set aside for at least ½ hour (ideally 1-2 hours).

Divide the dough in 10-12 equal pieces. Roll out into 5"-6" rounds, paint lightly with ghee, then prepare by one of the two following methods:

1) Make a slit from one edge of the round to the center. Wrap one cut edge around the other to make a cone-shape. Flatten the cone back into a disk, then roll out with the rolling pin to the thickness of cardboard, about 5"-6" wide.

2) Roll up the disk into a "jelly-roll." Now curl the roll into a spiral, like a cinnamon bun. Seal the outside end by pressing with your fingers, then flatten and roll out with a rolling pin to the thickness of cardboard, about 5"-6" wide.

Place the roti on a cake rack, and set on top of the oven rack in your oven; bake until lightly browned. Paint one side of the roti with ghee to keep it from becoming brittle.

You can also cook these in a skillet just like chapati. Remember to butter them when browned.

Makes 10-12
(traditional serving= 1)

Per serving: Calories: 84, Protein: 3 gm., Fat: 1.5 gm., Carbohydrates: 15 gm.

• • • •

Fresh Ingredients

Other Ingredients
Indian whole wheat flour, 2 cups
salt, 1 tsp
vegetable oil, 1 TBS
ghee, about ¼ cup

Spices

TOMATO PANCAKES
SPICY RICE AND CHICKPEA FLOUR PANCAKES WITH TOMATO

Makes 12
(traditional serving = 1)

*Per serving: Calories: 67,
Protein: 2 gm., Fat: 0 gm.,
Carbohydrates: 13 gm.*

• • • •

Fresh Ingredients
*tomato, ¼ cup
onion, 2 TBS
hot green pepper, ½ TBS
coriander leaves (cilantro),
   ½ TBS
garlic, ½ clove*

Other Ingredients
*chickpea flour, 1 cup
rice flour, ¾ cup
salt, 1 tsp
vegetable oil, for sautéing*

Spices
*cumin/coriander powder,
   1 TBS
oregano seeds (ajama), 1 tsp
turmeric, ½ tsp
cumin seeds, ¼ tsp
hot red pepper powder,
   ¼ tsp or to taste
hing, pinch*

Mix together to make a thin batter:

1 cup chickpea flour
¾ cup rice flour
¼ cup tomato, chopped
2 Tablespoons onion, chopped
1 Tablespoon cumin/coriander powder
½ Tablespoon fresh hot green pepper, chopped
½ Tablespoon fresh coriander leaves (cilantro),
   chopped
1 teaspoon salt
1 teaspoon oregano seeds (ajama)
½ teaspoon turmeric
¼ teaspoon cumin seeds
¼ teaspoon hot red pepper powder, or to taste
pinch hing
½ clove garlic, minced
1¾ cups warm water or more to make a thin
   batter

Pour ¼ cup onto a well-heated griddle. Sprinkle about a teaspoon of oil on the top of the pancake. Flip when browned on the first side. Brown lightly on the second side, fold in half, and remove from the pan. Repeat until all the batter is used up.

Serve this hot with *Yogurt Chutney*, pg. 48.

SWEET PARATHA SAUCE
SPICY SAUCE FOR DIPPING SWEET FILLED PARATHA

In a skillet, dry roast until just blackened, and set aside:
> 2 Tablespoons unsweetened coconut

In a bowl, combine, and set aside:
> 1½ cups cooking water from the split peas for
> *Sweet Filled Paratha*, pg. 77
> ¼-⅓ cup of the sweetened, pureed peas from the
> *Sweet Filled Paratha*, pg. 77
> a few whole, plain, cooked split yellow peas (opt.)

Combine in a blender:
> 1 Tablespoon fresh coriander leaves (cilantro),
> chopped
> 1½ teaspoons garam masala
> 1 teaspoon cumin seeds
> 1 teaspoon cumin/coriander powder
> 1 clove garlic, whole
> the blackened coconut

Add the blender mixture to the pea and water mixture, and set aside.

In a saucepan, heat:
> ½ Tablespoon vegetable oil
> pinch hing
> 1 teaspoon cumin/mustard/sesame seeds mixture

When the seeds pop, add:
> 1 teaspoon sugar
> 1 teaspoon salt
> ½ teaspoon turmeric

(cont.)

Makes about 2 cups
(traditional serving = 3 TBS)

*Per serving: Calories: 35,
Protein: 1 gm., Fat: 2 gm.,
Carbohydrates: 3 gm.*

• • • •

Fresh Ingredients
*coriander leaves (cilantro),
1 TBS
garlic, 1 clove*

Other Ingredients
*coconut, unsweetened
shredded, 2 TBS
⅓ cup sweet split pea puree
and water from cooking
split peas*
*vegetable oil, ½ TBS
sugar, 1 tsp
salt, 1 tsp*

**From Sweet Filled
Paratha, pg. 77*

(cont.)

½ teaspoon hot red pepper powder
¼ teaspoon coriander seeds
5 whole peppercorns
2-3 whole cardamoms
2-3 whole cloves
2-3 Indian bay leaves

Add the spiced pea sauce to the saucepan, and heat together. You may add more water for a thinner consistency, if desired.

GHEE
CLARIFIED BUTTER

Simmer until slightly brown, about 10-15 minutes:
1 pound unsalted butter

Skim off the foam, then pour off and save the clear layer on top--this is the ghee. Leave the grainy milk solids in the bottom of the pan. (For a treat, mix ½ Tablespoon sugar into the milk solids, and eat with a spoon.)

Ghee keeps a very long time in the refrigerator. You can soften it at room temperature or melt it as needed. Many Indian cooks traditionally keep ghee at room temperature for a shorter while, perhaps 4-6 months.

Makes 1¾ cups

Per Tablespoon: Calories: 117, Protein: 0 gm., Fat: 13 gm., Carbohydrates: 0 gm.

• • • •

Fresh Ingredients
butter, 1 lb unsalted

Other Ingredients

Spices

GRAINS

RICE DISHES

Eggplant Rice 84
With vegetables and spices

Khichadi 86
Rice with green mung beans

Rice Pilaf 87
Seasoned with sweet spices

Saffron Sweet Rice 88
Seasoned with saffron and sweetened with sugar

Spicy Rice 89
With hot spices, peanuts, and roasted chickpeas

Vegetable Biryani 90
Rice loaded with mixed vegetables

Soft Chawada 92
Rice flakes porridge

Yogurt Rice 93
Seasoned with spices and beans

OTHER GRAINS

Coriander Wada 94
Steamed and sautéed chickpea flour rounds

Pakora (Bhaji) 95
Spicy, deep-fried chickpea flour dumplings

Pithalay 96
Savory chickpea flour custard

Silk Wada 97
Chickpea flour and yogurt noodles

Uppama 99
Seasoned cream of wheat porridge

Wada 100
Fried whole wheat and chickpea flour rounds

Makes 5 cups
(traditional serving = ½ cup)

*Per serving: Calories: 96,
Protein: 1 gm., Fat: 3.8 gm.,
Carbohydrates: 14 gm.*

• • • •

Fresh Ingredients
*(optional: coriander leaves
(cilantro), 1½ TBS)
fresh hot pepper, ½ pepper
garlic, 1 clove
eggplant, 1 small
onion, ½ medium
tomato, medium, ½
(optional: peas, ¼ cup)*

Other Ingredients
*rice, ¾ cups uncooked
vegetable oil, 1½ TBS
salt, ½ tsp
coconut, unsweetened,
  garnish*

(cont.)

EGGPLANT RICE
RICE WITH EGGPLANT, VEGETABLES, AND SPICES

To make fresh masala, grind together and set aside:
> **1 Tablespoon fresh coriander leaves (cilantro)
> (opt.)**
> **1 teaspoon cumin/coriander powder**
> **½ teaspoon cinnamon**
> **½ fresh hot pepper**
> **1 clove garlic, chopped**
> **2 black peppercorns,
>   or pinch black pepper powder**
> **2 whole cloves,
>   or pinch ground cloves**
> **pinch ginger powder,
>   or ¾-inch cube fresh ginger, grated**

Bring to a boil in a small saucepan:
> **1½ cups water**
> **¾ cups uncooked rice**

Cover and reduce the heat to low. Cook 15-20 minutes, until all the water is absorbed. Do not stir while cooking, but you may fluff it gently with a fork when it is finished.

Heat in a saucepan:
> **1½ Tablespoons vegetable oil**
> **tiny pinch hing**
> **¼ teaspoon cumin/mustard/sesame seed
>   mixture**

When the seeds pop, add and sauté until the onions are transparent:
> **1 small eggplant, unpeeled, diced**
> **½ medium onion, diced**
> **½ medium tomato, diced**
> **¼ cup peas, fresh or frozen (opt.)**

Add:

     the fresh masala
     1 Tablespoon cumin/coriander powder
     ½ teaspoon hot red pepper powder
     ½ teaspoon salt
     ¼ teaspoon turmeric
     2-3 Indian bay leaves (opt.)

Continue to sauté until the eggplant is soft.

Separate the grains of cooked rice with a fork, and add to the sauté pan. Mix thoroughly and cook 3-5 minutes on low heat.

Sprinkle with:

     shredded, unsweetened coconut
     fresh, coriander leaves (cilantro), chopped (opt.)

Yogurt Soup, pg. 23, tastes wonderful spooned over the top of this dish.

Spices
cumin/coriander, 4 tsp
cinnamon, ground, ½ tsp
black peppercorns, 2 (or
  pinch ground)
cloves, 2 whole (or pinch
  ground)
ginger powder, pinch
hing, pinch
seeds mixture, ¼ tsp
hot red pepper powder,
  ½ tsp
turmeric, ¼ tsp
(optional: Indian bay
  leaves, 2-3)

KHICHADI
RICE WITH GREEN MUNG BEANS

Makes 4 cups
(traditional serving = ½ cup)

*Per serving: Calories: 66,
Protein: 1 gm., Fat: 0 gm.,
Carbohydrates: 14 gm.*

• • • •

Fresh Ingredients

Other Ingredients
*rice, uncooked, 1 cup
green, split mung dal,
    ½ cup
salt, ½ tsp*

Spices

Combine in a microwave-safe bowl, and microwave for
approximately 15 minutes:

> **2½ cups water**
> **1 cup uncooked rice, washed**
> **½ cup green, split mung dal (mung beans), washed**
> **½ teaspoon salt**

To make on the stove-top, combine the ingredients in a
saucepan, and bring to a boil. Reduce the heat to low, cover,
and let simmer undisturbed for 15-20 minutes, until all the
water is absorbed.

Optional additions:

> **½ teaspoon turmeric**
> **onion**
> **vegetables**
> **nuts**

Khichadi is especially good with *Yogurt Soup*, pg. 23,
spooned over the top.

RICE PILAF
RICE SEASONED WITH SWEET SPICES

Melt in a saucepan:
>   **2-3 Tablespoons unsalted butter**

Add whole spices:
>   **¾ teaspoon cumin seed**
>   **9 whole cloves**
>   **8-9 whole black peppercorns**
>   **5 whole cardamom seeds**
>   **3 Indian bay leaves**
>   **3 inches cinnamon stick, broken**

Add and sauté until transparent:
>   **3 medium onions, chopped**

Add:
>   **1½ cup uncooked basmati or other long-grain rice,**
>   **rinsed**
>   **1-1½ teaspoons salt**
>   **3 cups water**

Bring to a boil, then cover and simmer on low heat for 20-25 minutes, until the water is absorbed and the rice is soft. Do not stir.

When the rice is cooked, you may add for extra color and flavor:
>   **a pinch saffron**
>   **a pinch turmeric**
>   **fresh coriander leaves (cilantro)**
>   **cooked peas (opt.)**

Mix *very* gently. You may remove the whole spices before serving, or not; just advise your family or guests to avoid eating them.

Makes 5 cups
(traditional serving = ½ cup)

Per serving: Calories: 113, Protein: 2 gm., Fat: 3.3 gm., Carbohydrates: 19 gm.

• • • •

Fresh Ingredients
butter, unsalted, 2-3 TBS
onions, 3 medium
coriander leaves (cilantro),
    pinch
(optional: cooked peas)

Other Ingredients
basmati rice, 1½ cups
    uncooked
salt, 1-1½ tsp

Spices
cumin seeds, ¾ tsp
cloves, 9 whole
black peppercorns, 8-9 whole
cardamom seeds, 5 whole
bay leaves, 3
cinnamon stick, 3 inches
saffron, pinch
turmeric, pinch

SAFFRON SWEET RICE

RICE SEASONED WITH SAFFRON AND SWEETENED WITH SUGAR

Makes 5 cups
(traditional serving = ½ cup)

Per serving: Calories: 142,
Protein: 2 gm., Fat: 2 gm.,
Carbohydrates: 30 gm.

• • • •

Fresh Ingredients

Other Ingredients
basmati rice, 2 cups
  uncooked
sugar, ⅔ cup
ghee, 4 tsp

Spices
turmeric, ¼ tsp
saffron, ¼ tsp
cinnamon sticks, 2
cloves, 8-10
cardamoms, green, 8-10
  (1 tsp. cardamom powder)
black peppercorns, 8-10

In a saucepan, combine:
> **3½ cups water**
> **2 cups uncooked basmati rice**

Bring to a boil, cover, and simmer on low heat for 25-30 minutes, until the water is absorbed.

In a bowl, mix:
> **the cooked basmati rice (about 4 cups)**
> **⅔ cup sugar**
> **¼ teaspoon turmeric**
> **¼ teaspoon crushed saffron**

In a saucepan, melt:
> **4 teaspoons ghee**

Add to the saucepan and sauté:
> **2 cinnamon sticks, crushed or broken into**
> > **2-4 pieces**
> **8-10 whole cloves**
> **8-10 whole green cardamoms,**
> > **or 1 teaspoon cardamom powder**
> **8-10 whole black peppercorns**

When spice mixture "pops," add the rice mixture. Cover and sauté until warmed through.

You may remove the whole spices before serving, or not; just advise your family or guests to avoid eating them.

SPICY RICE
RICE WITH HOT SPICES, PEANUTS, AND ROASTED CHICKPEAS

In a saucepan, combine:
>   3½ cups water
>   2 cups uncooked basmati or other long-grain rice, rinsed

In a medium-sized bowl, combine:
>   the cooked rice (about 4 cups)
>   2 Tablespoons whole roasted Indian chickpeas
>   2 Tablespoons whole roasted peanuts

In a saucepan, heat:
>   1-2 Tablespoons vegetable oil
>   pinch hing
>   1 teaspoon cumin/mustard/sesame seed mixture

When the seeds pop, add and sauté until soft:
>   ½ cup onion, chopped
>   2 Tablespoons fresh coriander leaves (cilantro), chopped

Add:
>   1½ teaspoons cumin/coriander powder
>   1 teaspoon salt
>   1 teaspoon hot red pepper powder, or to taste
>   ½ teaspoon turmeric
>   ½ teaspoon sugar
>   juice from ¼-½ lime

Mix in the rice mixture, and heat until warmed through.

Makes 5 cups
(traditional serving = ½ cup)

Per serving: Calories: 116, Protein: 2 gm., Fat: 3 gm., Carbohydrates: 19 gm.

• • • •

Fresh Ingredients
*onion, ½ cup
coriander leaves (cilantro), 2 TBS
lime, ¼-½*

Other Ingredients
*basmati rice, 2 cups uncooked
roasted Indian chickpeas, 2 TBS
roasted peanuts, 2 TBS
vegetable oil, 1-2 TBS
salt, 1 tsp
sugar, ½ tsp*

Spices
*hing, pinch
seeds mixture, 1 tsp
cumin/coriander powder, 1½ tsp
hot red pepper powder, 1 tsp or to taste
turmeric, ½ tsp*

VEGETABLE BIRYANI
Rice, Loaded with Mixed Vegetables

Makes 5½ cups
(traditional serving = ½ cup)

*Per serving: Calories: 80,
Protein: 1 gm., Fat: 2.8 gm.,
Carbohydrates: 12 gm.*

••••

Fresh Ingredients
*potato, ½ medium
cauliflower, 1 floret
sweet red pepper, ¼
carrot, ½
eggplant, ¼ cup
hot green pepper, 1 small
coriander leaves (cilantro),
    1 TBS
coconut, 1 TBS
ginger, freshly grated, pinch
onion, ½
tomato, ½*

Other Ingredients
*vegetable oil, 1½ TBS
rice, uncooked, 1 cup
salt, 1 tsp*

(cont.)

In a large saucepan, heat:
>**1½ Tablespoons vegetable oil**
>**pinch hing**
>**½ teaspoon seeds mixture**
>**½ teaspoon cumin seeds**

When the seeds pop, add:
>**1 teaspoon hot red pepper powder**
>**1 teaspoon cumin/coriander powder**
>**½ teaspoon turmeric**
>**½ teaspoon garam masala**
>**¼-½ teaspoon Pav Bahji masala**

Add and bring to a boil:
>**2 cups water**
>**½ medium potato, chopped**
>**1 cauliflower floret, chopped**
>**¼ sweet red pepper, chopped**
>**½ carrot, peeled and sliced**
>**¼ cup eggplant, chopped**
>**1 small, fresh, hot green pepper, chopped**
>**1 Tablespoon fresh coriander leaves (cilantro),**
>   **chopped**
>**1 Tablespoon fresh coconut, chopped**
>**pinch freshly grated ginger**

Turn the heat to low, and add:
>**1 cup uncooked rice**
>**1 teaspoon salt**

Bring back to a boil over low heat, with the pot half-covered.
When this mixture is boiling, add:
>**½ onion, chopped**
>**½ tomato, chopped**

Simmer on low, half-covered, for 15-20 minutes, adding more water if needed (the mixture might still look damp.) Let sit a few minutes, then serve.

Spices

hing, pinch
seeds mixture, ½ tsp
cumin seeds, ½ tsp
hot red pepper powder, 1 tsp
cumin/coriander powder,
*   1 tsp*
turmeric, ½ tsp
garam masala, ½ tsp
Pav Bahji masala, ½ tsp

SOFT CHAWADA
RICE FLAKES PORRIDGE

Makes about 5 cups
(traditional serving = ½ cup)

Per serving: Calories: 284,
Protein: 5 gm., Fat: 7.3 gm.,
Carbohydrates: 48 gm.

• • • •

Fresh Ingredients
onion, ¾ cup
coriander leaves (cilantro),
*   3 TBS*
fresh hot pepper, 1½ TBS
(optional: lemon or lime
*   juice, 3 TBS)*

Other Ingredients
roasted rice flakes, (thin
*   poha), 4½ cups*
vegetable oil, ¼ cup
roasted peanuts, 3 TBS
roasted Indian chickpeas,
*   3 TBS*
salt, 1½ tsp
sugar, ¾ teaspoon

Spices
hing, pinch
seeds mixture, 1½ tsp
Indian bay leaves, 6-8
cumin/coriander powder,
*   1 TBS*
hot red pepper powder, 1 tsp
*   or to taste*
turmeric, ¾ tsp

In a bowl, measure out:
> **4½ cups roasted rice flakes (thin poha)**

Add just enough water to dampen, and set aside.

In a saucepan, heat:
> **¼ cup vegetable oil**
> **pinch hing**
> **1½ teaspoons cumin/mustard/sesame seed mixture**

When the seeds pop, add and sauté until the onion is soft:
> **¾ cup onion, chopped**
> **3 Tablespoons fresh coriander leaves (cilantro), chopped**
> **1½ Tablespoons fresh hot pepper, chopped**
> **6-8 Indian bay leaves**

Add:
> **3 Tablespoons roasted peanuts, in halves**
> **3 Tablespoons roasted Indian chickpeas, whole**

Now add:
> **1 Tablespoon cumin/coriander powder**
> **1½ teaspoon salt**
> **1 teaspoon hot red pepper powder, or to taste**
> **¾ teaspoon turmeric**
> **¾ teaspoon sugar**
> **3 Tablespoons lemon or lime juice (opt.)**

Finally, add:
> **the dampened rice flakes**

The mixture should be like thick, cooked cream of wheat cereal. If it is too dry, add 1 or 2 Tablespoons water. Turn the heat to low, cover tightly, cook for 5-6 minutes and serve immediately.

YOGURT RICE

RICE SEASONED WITH YOGURT, SPICES, AND BEANS

In a saucepan, combine:

2⅔ cups water
1½ cup uncooked basmati or other long-grain rice, rinsed

Bring to a boil, cover, and turn the heat to low. Simmer undisturbed for 15-20 minutes until the liquid has been absorbed.

In a large bowl, mix together:

the cooked basmati rice (3 cups), cooled and with grains separated by hand
¾ cup plain yogurt (more if needed for smoother consistency)
¼ teaspoon milk (more if needed for thinner consistency)

In a small saucepan, heat:

1 Tablespoon vegetable oil
pinch hing
1 teaspoon cumin/mustard/sesame seeds mixture

Add and sauté until lightly browned:

1 Tablespoon roasted Indian chick peas
1 Tablespoon roasted peanuts, whole
1 Tablespoon fresh coriander leaves (cilantro), chopped
1 Tablespoon fresh hot green pepper, chopped
1 teaspoon urad dal, dry
1 teaspoon chana dal, dry
4-5 Indian bay leaves

Mix in:

2 teaspoons cumin/coriander powder
1 teaspoon salt
¼ teaspoon turmeric
¼ teaspoon hot red pepper powder

(cont.)

Makes 4 cups
(traditional serving = ½ cup)

Per serving: Calories: 114,
Protein: 3 gm., Fat: 3.2 gm.,
Carbohydrates: 18 gm.

• • • •

Fresh Ingredients
yogurt, ¾ cup plain
milk, ¼ tsp
coriander leaves (cilantro),
* 1 TBS*
hot green pepper, 1 TBS

Other Ingredients
basmati rice, uncooked,
* 1½ cups*
vegetable oil, 1 TBS
roasted Indian chickpeas,
* 1 TBS*
roasted peanuts, 1 TBS
urad dal, 1 tsp
chana dal, 1 tsp
salt, 1 tsp
sugar, pinch

Spices
hing, pinch
seeds mixture, 1 tsp
Indian bay leaves, 4-5
cumin/coriander powder, 2 tsp
turmeric, ¼ tsp
hot red pepper powder, ¼ tsp

Remove the saucepan from the heat, and add its contents to the rice mixture.

Add and mix well:
    pinch of sugar

CORIANDER WADA
STEAMED AND SAUTÉED CHICKPEA FLOUR ROUNDS

Makes about 1 cup
(traditional serving = 2 TBS)

*Per serving: Calories: 91,
Protein: 2 gm., Fat: 5.6 gm.,
Carbohydrates: 7 gm.*

• • • •

Fresh Ingredients
*coriander leaves (cilantro),
  ½ cup*

Other Ingredients
*chickpea flour, 1 cup
vegetable oil, 3 TBS
salt, 1 tsp
sesame seeds, 1½ tsp*

Spices
*cumin/coriander powder,
  2 tsp
hot red pepper powder,
  ½ tsp
turmeric, ½ tsp
hing, 2 pinches
seeds mixture, ¼ tsp*

In a bowl, mix together:
    1 cup chickpea flour
    ½ cup fresh coriander leaves (cilantro), chopped
    2 teaspoons cumin/coriander powder
    1 teaspoon salt
    ½ teaspoon sesame seeds
    ½ teaspoon hot red pepper powder
    ½ teaspoon turmeric
    pinch hing
    2 Tablespoons vegetable oil

Add about 1½ cups warm water, a little at a time, enough to make a slightly sticky dough. With wet hands, roll into small sausage-shapes. Cook 20-25 minutes under medium pressure in a pressure cooker, or by another method (such as steaming) until a sharp knife poked through the dough comes out clean. Slice into rounds about ¼" thick.

In a saucepan or frying pan, heat:
    1 Tablespoon vegetable oil
    pinch hing
    1 teaspoon sesame seeds
    ¼ teaspoon cumin/mustard/sesame seed mixture

When the seeds pop, add the rounds to the saucepan, mix, and add more salt to taste. Serve.

PAKORA (BHAJI)
Spicy, Deep-fried Chickpea Flour Dumplings

In a bowl, mix:
> **6 Tablespoons rice flour**
> **2¼ cups chickpea flour**

Add spices:
> **1½ teaspoons salt**
> **¾ teaspoon oregano seeds (ajama)**
> **¾ teaspoon hot red pepper powder (opt.)**
> **¾ teaspoon cumin seeds**
> **¾ teaspoon cumin/coriander powder**
> **¼-½ teaspoon turmeric**
> **⅛ teaspoon baking soda**

Mix in:
> **2¼ cups water or enough to make a thick batter**

Add:
> **3 small onions, coarsely chopped**
> **1 fresh hot pepper, chopped large**
> **1½ Tablespoons cauliflower, chopped (or other raw veg., eg. spinach)**
> **1½ Tablespoons fresh coriander, chopped**

Stir well to combine, then *remove the large hot pepper pieces.* Heat some oil in a deep fryer, fry the mixture 1 Tablespoonful at a time, and drain.

These may be served with *Apple Butter Chutney*, pg. 36, or *Coriander Chutney*, pg. 38.

Makes 24-27
(traditional serving = 2-3)

Per serving: Calories: 111, Protein: 4 gm., Fat: 1 gm., Carbohydrates: 20 gm.

• • • •

Fresh Ingredients
onions, 3 small
fresh hot pepper, 1
cauliflower, 1½ TBS
coriander leaves (cilantro), 1½ TBS

Other Ingredients
rice flour, 6 TBS
chickpea flour, 2¼ cups
salt, 1½ tsp
baking soda, ⅛ tsp
vegetable oil, for deep frying

Spices
oregano seeds (ajama), ¾ tsp
hot red pepper powder, ¾ tsp (opt.)
cumin seeds, ¾ tsp
cumin/coriander powder, ¾ tsp
turmeric, ¼-½ tsp

PITHALAY

SAVORY CHICKPEA FLOUR CUSTARD

Makes 3½ cups
(traditional serving = 3 TBS)

Per serving: Calories: 32,
Protein: 1 gm., Fat: 1.6 gm.,
Carbohydrates: 3 gm.

• • • •

Fresh Ingredients
onion, ⅓ cup
hot pepper, 1 TBS
(optional: garlic, 1 clove)
coriander leaves (cilantro),
* 2 TBS*

Other Ingredients
chickpea flour, 1 cup
vegetable oil, 2 TBS
salt, 1 teaspoon

Spices
hing, pinch
seeds mixture, 1 tsp
Indian bay leaves, 3-4
cumin/coriander powder,
* 1½ tsp*
turmeric, ½ tsp
hot red pepper powder, pinch

In a small bowl combine into a wet paste:
>**1 cup chickpea flour**
>**¾-1 cup water**

In a saucepan, heat:
>**2 Tablespoons vegetable oil**
>**pinch hing**
>**1 teaspoon cumin/mustard/sesame seed mixture**

When the seeds pop, add:
>**⅓ cup onion, chopped**
>**1 Tablespoon chopped fresh hot pepper**
>**3-4 Indian bay leaves**
>**1 clove garlic, minced (opt.)**

When the onion becomes transparent, add:
>**1½ teaspoon cumin/coriander powder**
>**½ teaspoon turmeric**
>**pinch hot red pepper powder, or to taste**

Now add:
>**3 cups water**
>**2 Tablespoons fresh coriander leaves (cilantro),**
>   **chopped**
>**1 teaspoon salt**

Bring this mixture to a brisk boil. Stir in the chickpea flour paste, stirring quickly and completely. Turn the heat as low as possible, cover, and heat for 2-3 minutes. The mixture will thicken to a soft pudding consistency.

This is best served in individual bowls with *Corn Chapati*, pg. 67, and rice, and is one of Sunetra's favorite dishes.

SILK WADA

SILKEN CHICKPEA FLOUR AND YOGURT NOODLES

Grease the outside bottoms of as many large, flat metal pans as you can find (3 very large pans is ideal). You can use pizza pans, cookie sheets, baking pans, etc.

In a small mixing bowl or pitcher, combine until smooth:
> ½ cup plain yogurt
> 1 cup water

In a separate bowl, place:
> ½ cup chickpea flour

Add the yogurt mixture to the flour, little by little, and mix until smooth.

Mix in:
> ¼ teaspoon salt
> ½ teaspoon cumin/coriander powder
> ¼ teaspoon turmeric

Pour this mixture into a heavy saucepan, and heat over medium to low, *stirring constantly*, until it is as thick as pudding—about 5-8 minutes. Make sure the batter doesn't stick to the bottom or sides of the pan, and smooth out any lumps. Then cover and let sit over *very* low heat for about 1 minute. Remove from the heat and let sit, still covered, for 3 more minutes.

Working quickly so that the batter does not get too thick, spoon about 3-4 Tablespoons of batter onto each greased surface, and smooth over to cover the surface *very* thinly. Let dry for about 5 minutes. Then score each surface into 1¼" strips, and roll each strip into little "jelly rolls" called "wada." Place each roll onto an ungreased platter.

Makes about 24
(traditional serving = 2)

*Per serving: Calories: 32,
Protein: 1 gm., Fat: 1.8 gm.,
Carbohydrates: 3 gm.*

• • • •

Fresh Ingredients
*yogurt, plain, ½ cup
coriander leaves (cilantro),
   1 TBS*

Other Ingredients
*chickpea flour, ½ cup
salt, ¼ tsp
vegetable oil, 1 TBS
coconut, unsweetened,
   ½ TBS*

Spices
*cumin/coriander powder,
   ½ tsp
turmeric, ¼ tsp
hing, a pinch
seeds mixture, ½ TBS
sesame seeds, ½ TBS
oregano seeds (ajama),
   ¼-½ TBS*

Sprinkle with:
> ½ Tablespoon shredded, unsweetened coconut

In a small frying pan, heat:
> **1 Tablespoon vegetable oil**
> **pinch hing**
> **½ Tablespoon cumin/mustard/sesame seed mixture**
> **½ Tablespoon sesame seeds**
> **¼-½ Tablespoon oregano seeds (ajama)**
> **1 Tablespoon fresh coriander leaves (cilantro) chopped**

When the seeds pop, remove from the heat and pour over the wada.

Traditionally this is eaten as finger food, perhaps with *Sweet Filled Paratha*, pg. 77, or a sweet dessert.

UPPAMA
SEASONED CREAM OF WHEAT PORRIDGE

Dry roast in a skillet until lightly browned, about 5 minutes:
  1 cup uncooked cream of wheat

Set aside.

Heat in a saucepan:
  1 Tablespoon vegetable oil

Add and heat until the seeds pop:
  pinch hing
  1 teaspoon cumin/mustard/sesame seed mixture

Add and bring to a boil:
  2 cups water
  ½ cup tomato, chopped
  ½ cup onion, chopped
  1 Tablespoon urad dal ("black" lentils)
  1 Tablespoon chana dal (yellow split peas)
  1 Tablespoon fresh coriander leaves (cilantro),
      chopped
  2 teaspoons cumin/coriander powder
  1 teaspoon hot red pepper powder
  1 teaspoon salt
  ½ teaspoon turmeric
  ½ of one fresh hot green pepper, chopped
  4 or 5 bay leaves

As the mixture is boiling, add:
  the roasted cream of wheat
  juice of ¼ lemon

Cover and simmer a few minutes until very thick.

Serve sprinkled with:
  shredded unsweetened coconut

Makes about 4 cups
(traditional serving = ½ cup)

*Per serving: Calories: 84,
Protein: 2 gm., Fat: 1.7 gm.,
Carbohydrates: 15 gm.*

• • • •

Fresh Ingredients
*tomato, ½ cup
onion, ½ cup
coriander leaves (cilantro),
  1 TBS
hot green pepper, ½
juice of ¼ lemon*

Other Ingredients
*cream of wheat, uncooked,
  1 cup
vegetable oil, 1 TBS
urad dal, 1 TBS
chana dal, 1 TBS
salt, 1 tsp
coconut, unsweetened, for
  garnish*

Spices
*hing, pinch
seeds mixture, 1 tsp
cumin/coriander powder,
  2 tsp
hot red pepper powder, 1 tsp
turmeric, ½ tsp
Indian bay leaves, 4-5*

WADA

FRIED WHOLE WHEAT AND CHICKPEA FLOUR ROUNDS

Makes 10
(traditional serving = 1)

*Per serving: Calories: 39,
Protein: 2 gm., Fat: .4 gm.,
Carbohydrates: 7 gm.*

• • • •

Fresh Ingredients
*coriander leaves (cilantro),
½ TBS*

Other Ingredients
*Indian whole wheat flour,
¾ cup
chickpea flour, ¼ cup
sesame seeds, ½ TBS
salt, ½ tsp
vegetable oil for deep frying*

Spices
*cumin/coriander powder,
1 tsp
turmeric, ¼ tsp
hot red pepper powder,
¼ tsp or to taste
hing, pinch*

In a medium-sized bowl, combine well by hand:
    ¾ cup Indian whole wheat flour
    ¼ cup chickpea flour
    **½ Tablespoon fresh coriander leaves (cilantro),
      chopped**
    ½ Tablespoon sesame seeds
    1 teaspoon cumin/coriander powder
    ½ teaspoon salt
    ¼ teaspoon turmeric
    ¼ teaspoon hot red pepper powder, or to taste
    pinch hing

Add about ⅔ cup water, enough to make a sticky dough.

Lay a very wet paper towel on the counter. With wet fingers, press balls of dough into pancakes of cardboard thickness.

Deep fry in oil until browned, then drain on paper towels.

DALS & LEGUMES

BLACK-EYED PEA CURRY

SEASONED BLACK-EYED PEAS WITH ONIONS AND TOMATO

Makes 3½ cups
(traditional serving = 3 TBS)

*Per serving: Calories: 30,
Protein: 1 gm., Fat: 0.8 gm.,
Carbohydrates: 5 gm.*

• • • •

Fresh Ingredients
*jalapeño pepper, ½
garlic, ½ clove
ginger, ¼ inch grated
onions, 2 medium
tomatoes, 1½
coriander leaves (cilantro),
   2 TBS*

Other Ingredients
*vegetable oil, 1 TBS
(optional: tomato paste,
   1 TBS)
black-eyed peas, ⅔ cup raw
   (or 1⅓ cups cooked)
salt, 1¼ tsp*

(cont.)

Cook **1 cup raw black-eyed peas** by placing them in a saucepan with enough water to cover, bringing to a boil and discarding the water 2 times. Then add 3 cups water again, bring to a boil, and simmer until the peas are soft, about 45 minutes. Drain and set aside.

Make a hot pepper mixture by grinding together and setting aside:

> **½ jalapeño pepper**
> **½ clove garlic, minced**
> **¼ inch fresh ginger, grated**
> **pinch cumin seeds**

Heat in a saucepan:

> **1 Tablespoon vegetable oil**
> **tiny pinch hing**
> **½ teaspoon cumin/mustard/sesame seed
>   mixture**

When the seeds pop, add and sauté until the onions are soft:

> **2 medium onions, diced**
> **1½ tomatoes, diced**
> **the hot pepper mixture**
> **1 Tablespoon tomato paste (opt.)**

Add powdered spices and whole spices:

> **2 teaspoons cumin/coriander powder**
> **1 teaspoon turmeric**
> **1 teaspoon garam masala**

¼-½ teaspoon hot red pepper powder (opt.)
6 whole cloves
10 black peppers
2 inch cinnamon stick, broken into pieces
1 Tablespoon Indian bay leaves

Then add:
the cooked black-eyed peas (about 1½ cups)
⅔ cup water
2 Tablespoons fresh coriander leaves, chopped.
1¼ teaspoon salt

Simmer for 10 minutes. Serve hot.

Spices
cumin seeds, pinch
hing, pinch
seeds mixture, ½ tsp
cumin/coriander powder,
  2 tsp
turmeric, 1 tsp
garam masala, 1 tsp
(optional: hot red pepper
  powder, ¼-½ tsp)
cloves, whole, 6
black peppercorns, whole, 10
cinnamon stick, 2 inches
Indian bay leaves, 1 TBS

CHANA
SEASONED CHICKPEAS WITH ONIONS AND TOMATO

Makes 4 cups
(traditional serving = 3 TBS)

Per serving: Calories: 34, Protein: 1 gm., Fat: 0.9 gm., Carbohydrates: 5 gm.

• • • •

Fresh Ingredients
jalapeño pepper, ½
garlic, ½ clove
ginger, ¼ inch grated
onions, 2
tomato, 1½ medium
coriander leaves (cilantro), 2 TBS

Other Ingredients
vegetable oil, 1 TBS
(optional: tomato paste, 1 TBS)
chickpeas, 1¾ cups cooked (or 1[19 oz.] can)
salt, 1¼ tsp

Spices
cumin seeds, pinch
hing, pinch
seeds mixture, ½ tsp
cumin/coriander powder, 2 tsp
turmeric powder, 1 tsp
garam masala, 1 tsp
(cont.)

Make a hot pepper mixture by grinding together and setting aside:

> ½ jalapeño pepper
> ½ clove garlic, minced
> ¼ inch fresh ginger, grated
> pinch cumin seeds

Heat in a saucepan:

> 1 Tablespoons vegetable oil
> tiny pinch hing
> ½ teaspoon cumin/mustard/sesame seed mixture

When the seeds pop, add and sauté until the onions are soft:

> 2 medium onions, diced
> 1½ tomatoes, diced
> the hot pepper mixture
> 1 Tablespoon tomato paste (opt.)

Add powdered spices and whole spices:

> 2 teaspoons cumin/coriander powder
> 1 teaspoon turmeric
> 1 teaspoon garam masala
> ¼-½ teaspoon hot red pepper powder (opt.)
> 6 whole cloves
> 10 black peppers
> 2 inch cinnamon stick, broken into pieces
> 1 Tablespoon bay leaves

Then add:

> 1¾ cups cooked chickpeas (1 [19 oz.] can)
> ⅔ cup water
> 1¼ teaspoon salt
> 2 Tablespoons fresh coriander leaves (cilantro), chopped

(cont.)

Simmer for 10 minutes. Serve hot. You can crush a few chickpeas against the side of the pot with your spoon to thicken the sauce.

HOT CHANA
CHICKPEAS WITH VERY HOT SPICES

In a bowl, cover with water and soak overnight:
> **1 cup dry Indian chickpeas (can substitute other chickpeas)**

Drain and cook the soaked beans in enough fresh water to cover until soft, not mushy. Set aside with their cooking liquid.

In a saucepan, heat:
> **1 Tablespoon vegetable oil**
> **pinch hing**
> **1 teaspoon cumin/mustard/sesame seed mixture**

When the seeds pop, add:
> **¼ cup onion, chopped**
> **3 Indian bay leaves**
> **2 Tablespoons fresh coriander leaves (cilantro), chopped**
> **1 clove garlic, minced (opt.)**

When the onion becomes transparent, add the dry spices:
> **1 teaspoon cumin/coriander powder**
> **1 teaspoon salt**
> **½-1 teaspoon hot red pepper powder**
> **½ teaspoon turmeric**
> **½ teaspoon garam masala**

Add the cooked chickpeas and a small amount of their cooking liquid. Mix well and serve. This is best served with *Puri*, pg. 71.

Spices (cont.)
(optional: hot red pepper powder, ¼-½ tsp)
cloves, whole, 6
black peppercorns, whole, 10
cinnamon stick, 2 inches
Indian bay leaves, 1 TBS

Makes 2 cups
(traditional serving = 3 TBS)

Per serving: Calories: 63, Protein: 2 gm., Fat: 1.8 gm., Carbohydrates: 9 gm.

• • • •

Fresh Ingredients
onion, ¼ cup
coriander leaves (cilantro), 2 TBS
(optional: garlic, 1 clove)

Other Ingredients
chickpeas, dried, 1 cup
salt, 1 tsp
vegetable oil, 1 TBS

Spices
hing, pinch
seeds mixture, 1 tsp
Indian bay leaves, 3
turmeric, ½ tsp
cumin/coriander powder, 1 tsp
hot red pepper powder, ½-1 tsp
garam masala, ½ tsp

KHAMONG DHOKLA
STEAMED SPLIT PEA BREAD

Soak about **1½ cups yellow split peas** in enough water to cover for at least 1 hour (preferably 6 hours or overnight). Drain and puree.

Mix by hand in a bowl:
> **3½ cups pureed split peas (as above)**
> **1½ Tablespoons yogurt mixed with ¼ cup water**
> **1½ teaspoon salt**
> **1 teaspoon turmeric**
> **1 teaspoon baking soda**
> **1 jalapeño pepper, minced**
> **1 clove garlic, ground**
> **½ inch cube of ginger, grated**
> **pinch cumin seeds**

This mixture should taste slightly sour; add more yogurt if you want to increase the sour flavor.

Grease the bottom of a pressure cooker or 8"-9" steamer pan. Pour in the mixture to about 1-1½ inches high (thick). Steam until cooked through—20-25 minutes under pressure, 45 minutes over steam. With a blunt knife or spatula, scrape around the edge of the pan, and cut the cooked mixture into 1½" diamonds. Turn out onto a serving plate.

Heat in a small saucepan:
> **1½ Tablespoons vegetable oil**
> **pinch hing**
> **1 teaspoon cumin/mustard/sesame seed mixture**
> **1 teaspoon sesame seeds**
> **½ teaspoon oregano seeds (ajama)**
> **2 Tablespoons fresh coriander leaves (cilantro), chopped**

When the seeds pop, remove from the heat and pour over the dhokla diamonds, shaking to mix.

(cont.)

Makes 10-12
(traditional serving = 1)

Per serving: Calories: 81, Protein: 4 gm., Fat: 2 gm., Carbohydrates: 12 gm.

• • • •

Fresh Ingredients
yogurt, 1½ TBS
jalapeño pepper, 1
garlic, 1 clove
ginger, ½ inch cube
coriander leaves (cilantro), 2 TBS
hot green peppers to taste

Other Ingredients
split yellow peas, 1½ cups dry
salt, 1½ tsp or more to taste
baking soda, 1 tsp
vegetable oil, 1½ TBS
sesame seeds, 1 tsp

Spices
turmeric, 1 tsp
cumin seeds, pinch
hing, pinch
seeds mixture, 1 tsp
oregano seeds (ajama), ½ tsp

For a hot topping, sauté briefly in a few drops of oil:
fresh, green hot peppers, chopped
salt to taste

LENTILS WITH DILL
LENTILS WITH FRESH DILL AND OTHER SPICES

Prepare the beans (you will need 1 cup of prepared beans),
Either: boil **oily lentils** for 20-25 minutes, or
              soak **green mung beans** for 20-60 minutes,
              or soak **plain lentils** for 20-60 minutes

Heat:
1 Tablespoon vegetable oil

Add:

pinch hing
¼ teaspoon cumin/mustard/sesame seed mixture
3-4 Indian bay leaves
2 dried hot peppers
¼ teaspoon turmeric

When the seeds pop, add and stir well:
1 cup fresh dill, chopped
1 cup prepared beans (see above)
1 teaspoon cumin/coriander powder
¼ teaspoon salt
¼ teaspoon hot red pepper powder (opt.)
2 Tablespoons fresh coriander leaves (cilantro),
    chopped
¼ cup water

Cover and simmer the oily lentils or mung beans for 10 minutes, or the plain lentils 20 minutes, until the beans are tender.

Makes 2½ cups
(traditional serving = 2 TBS)

Per serving: Calories: 18, Protein: 1 gm., Fat: 0.7 gm., Carbohydrates: 2 gm.

• • • •

Fresh Ingredients
dill, 1 cup fresh
coriander leaves (cilantro),
*   2 TBS*

Other Ingredients
lentils, oily (or other),
*   ½ cup dry*
vegetable oil, 1 TBS
salt, ¼ tsp

Spices
hing, pinch
seeds mixture, ¼ tsp
Indian bay leaves, 3-4
dried hot peppers, 2
turmeric, ¼ tsp
cumin/coriander powder,
*   1 tsp*
(optional: hot red pepper
*   powder, ¼ tsp)*

LENTILS WITH SCALLIONS

LENTILS WITH SCALLIONS AND SPICES

Makes 1½-2 cups
(traditional serving = 2 TBS)

*Per serving: Calories: 26,
Protein: 1 gm., Fat: 0.9 gm.,
Carbohydrates: 3 gm.*

• • • •

Fresh Ingredients
*scallions, 1 cup
garlic, 1 clove
onion, 1 TBS
coriander leaves (cilantro),
    1 TBS
fresh Indian bay leaves, 3*

Other Ingredients
*lentils, oily (or other), ½ cup
    dry
vegetable oil, 1 TBS
salt, 1 tsp*

Spices
*hing, pinch
seeds mixture, ½ tsp
cumin/coriander powder,
    1 tsp
garam masala, ½ tsp
turmeric, ½ tsp
Pav Bahji masala, ½ tsp
hot red pepper powder,
    ¼-½ tsp*

In a saucepan, place:
> ½ cup oily lentils (or yellow lentils or mung
>   beans)
> ½ cup water

Partially cover the beans and simmer about 20 minutes; the beans will only be cooked somewhat. Check on them now and then, and add a little more water if they are getting too dry. They should be soft on the outside but hard in the center. Set them aside in their water.

In another saucepan, heat:
> 1 Tablespoon vegetable oil
> pinch hing
> ½ teaspoon cumin/mustard/sesame seed mixture

When the seeds pop, add:
> 1 cup chopped scallions
> 1 clove garlic, chopped
> 1 Tablespoon chopped onion
> 1 Tablespoon fresh coriander leaves (cilantro),
>   chopped
> 3 Indian bay leaves, fresh if possible
> 1 teaspoon cumin/coriander powder
> 1 teaspoon salt
> ½ teaspoon garam masala
> ½ teaspoon turmeric
> ½ teaspoon Pav Bahji masala
> ¼-½ teaspoon hot red pepper powder

Add the lentils and their water. Simmer covered or uncovered for about 10 minutes until the beans are tender, adding more water as needed to keep the mixture from sticking to the pan.

PEANUT VEGETABLE
RAW PEANUTS, STEAMED AND SPICED

Boil in a small saucepan with 2 cups water for 10-15 minutes, or cook under medium pressure for about 15 minutes until soft:

>**1 cup raw peanuts (preferably Indian peanuts)**
>**1-2 cups water (enough for peanuts to float)**

Drain the peanuts. In another small saucepan, heat:

>**1 Tablespoon vegetable oil**
>**pinch hing**
>**½ teaspoon cumin/mustard/sesame seed mixture**
>**1 dried hot pepper**

When the seeds pop, add and cook until the onions are soft:

>**1 teaspoon cumin/coriander powder**
>**½ teaspoon turmeric**
>**½ teaspoon garam masala**
>**½ teaspoon salt**
>**¼-½ teaspoon hot red pepper powder (opt.)**
>**½ cup onion, chopped**
>**1 teaspoon fresh coriander (cilantro), chopped**

Add the peanuts and 1/4 cup water. Heat and eat.

Makes 1½ cups
(traditional serving = 2-3 TBS)

Per serving: Calories: 43,
Protein: 2 gm., Fat: 1.4 gm.,
Carbohydrates: 6 gm.

• • • •

Fresh Ingredients
onion, ½ cup
coriander leaves (cilantro),
*   1 tsp*

Other Ingredients
peanuts, raw, 1 cup (Indian
*   peanuts preferably)*
vegetable oil, 1 TBS
salt, ½ tsp

Spices
hing, pinch
seeds mixture, ½ tsp
dried hot pepper, 1
cumin/coriander powder,
*   1 tsp*
turmeric, ½ tsp
garam masala, ½ tsp
(optional: hot red pepper
*   powder, ¼-½ tsp)*

RADISH AND MUNG BEANS

MUNG BEANS WITH DAIKON RADISH AND SPICES

Makes 2½ cups
(traditional serving = 2 TBS)

Per serving: Calories: 31, Protein: 1 gm., Fat: 0.7 gm., Carbohydrates: 4 gm.

• • • •

Fresh Ingredients
daikon radish, 1 cup
coriander leaves (cilantro), 2 TBS
lime (or lemon) juice, 1 TBS

Other Ingredients
yellow mung beans, dry, 1 cup
vegetable oil, 1 TBS
salt, 1 tsp
sugar, ½ tsp

Spices
hing, pinch
seeds mixture, 1 tsp
cumin/coriander powder, 2 tsp
turmeric powder, 1 tsp
garam masala, 1 tsp
hot red pepper powder, ½-¾ tsp

In a bowl, soak overnight (or for at least for 20 minutes) in enough water to cover:
> **1 cup dry yellow mung beans**

Drain off the water and add:
> **1 cup fresh daikon radish, shredded**

In a saucepan, heat:
> **1 Tablespoon vegetable oil**
> **pinch hing**
> **1 teaspoon cumin/mustard/sesame seed mixture**

When the seeds pop, add:
> **2 Tablespoons fresh coriander leaves (cilantro), chopped**
> **2 teaspoons cumin/coriander powder**
> **1 teaspoon turmeric**
> **1 teaspoon garam masala**
> **1 teaspoon salt**
> **½-¾ teaspoon hot red pepper powder**

Add:
> **the radish and bean mixture**
> **½ teaspoon sugar**
> **1 Tablespoon lime or lemon juice**

Cover and simmer over low heat without adding water, stirring occasionally, for 10 minutes or until the beans are cooked.

SPICY MUNG BEAN CURRY

Seasoned Green Mung Beans

In a saucepan, cook for 10 minutes until soft:
> **1 cup green mung beans**
> **1 cup of water**

Set aside the beans in their cooking water.

In another saucepan, heat:
> **1 Tablespoon vegetable oil**
> **pinch hing**
> **1 teaspoon cumin/mustard/sesame seed mixture**

When seeds pop, add:
> **2½ Tablespoons onion, chopped**
> **1 Tablespoon tomato, chopped**
> **pinch fresh jalapeño pepper, chopped**
> **pinch fresh garlic cloves, chopped**
> **½ cup canned crushed tomatoes (or tomato puree)**
> **1 teaspoon grated fresh ginger**
> **1 Tablespoon cumin/coriander powder**
> **1½-2 teaspoons salt (to taste)**
> **1 teaspoon garam masala**
> **½ teaspoon Pav Bahji masala**
> **½ teaspoon turmeric**
> **¼ teaspoon hot red pepper powder (opt.)**

Add the mung beans and their water, and heat through. Add a little more water if necessary, but the consistency should be thick.

Top with:
> **1½-2 Tablespoons butter**
> **1 Tablespoon fresh coriander leaves (cilantro), chopped**

This is best with rice and/or pita bread. This dish freezes well.

Makes 2¼ cups
(traditional serving = 2 TBS)

Per serving: Calories: 38, Protein: 1 gm., Fat: 1.6 gm., Carbohydrates: 4 gm.

• • • •

Fresh Ingredients
onion, 2½ TBS
tomato, 1 TBS
jalapeño pepper, pinch
garlic, pinch
ginger, 1 tsp
butter, unsalted, 1½-2 TBS
coriander leaves (cilantro), 1 TBS

Other Ingredients
green mung beans, whole, 1 cup dry
vegetable oil, 1 TBS
canned crushed tomato, ½ cup
salt, 1½-2 tsp

Spices
hing, pinch
seeds mixture, 1 tsp
cumin/coriander powder, 1 TBS
garam masala, 1 tsp
Pav Bahji masala, ½ tsp
turmeric, ½ tsp
(optional: hot red pepper powder, ¼ tsp)

SPINACH DAL

LENTILS WITH SPINACH, PEANUTS, AND SPICES

Makes 1½-2 cups
(traditional serving = 2 TBS)

Per serving: Calories: 29,
Protein: 1 gm., Fat: 1.1 gm.,
Carbohydrates: 3 gm.

• • • •

Fresh Ingredients
spinach, fresh, ¼ cup, or
  2 TBS frozen
(optional: tomatoes, broccoli,
  or green pepper, 2-4 Tbs)
onion, ¼
tomato, ½
(optional: coriander leaves
  (cilantro) to taste)
garlic, ½ clove

Other Ingredients
lentils, oily (or other), ½ cup
peanuts, raw, ½ TBS
vegetable oil, 1 TBS
salt, ½ tsp and more to taste
(optional: tomato paste,
  ½ TBS)

(cont.)

Combine in a small saucepan:
> ¼ cup fresh spinach,
>> or 2 Tablespoons frozen spinach, thawed, and
>> drained
>
> ½ cup oily (or other) yellow lentils
> ½ Tablespoon raw, whole peanuts
> ¼ teaspoon turmeric
> ½ dried hot pepper
> ½ teaspoon salt
> 2-4 Tablespoons tomatoes, broccoli, green pepper
>> (opt.)
>
> about ½ cup water

Cook for 15 minutes, adding more water if necessary to keep mixture liquid. Puree in a blender or with an egg-beater, and set aside in a bowl.

In a pan, heat:
> 1 Tablespoon vegetable oil

Add:
> ¼ teaspoon cumin/mustard/sesame seed mixture

When the seeds pop, add and sauté:
> ¼ onion, chopped
> ½ tomato, chopped
> fresh coriander leaves (cilantro), (opt.)
> ½ Tablespoon tomato paste (opt.)

Then add and continue cooking:
> ½ clove garlic, chopped
> ½ Tablespoon cumin/coriander powder

¼ teaspoon hot red pepper powder (opt.)
¼ teaspoon garam masala
¼ teaspoon Pav Bahji masala
salt to taste

Add the spinach/lentil mixture to the spices, and remove from the heat. Add water as needed to thin the consistency.

Spices
turmeric, ¼ tsp
dried hot pepper, ½
seeds mixture, ¼ tsp
cumin/coriander powder,
   ½ TBS
(optional: hot red pepper
   powder, ¼ tsp)
garam masala, ¼ tsp
Pav Bahji masala, ¼ tsp

SPROUTED MUNG BEAN VEGETABLE

SPROUTED MUNG BEANS WITH COCONUT AND SPICES

Makes 2½ cups
(traditional serving = 2 TBS)

*Per serving: Calories: 20,
Protein: 0 gm., Fat: 1.4 gm.,
Carbohydrates: 1 gm.*

• • • •

Fresh Ingredients
onion, 1 medium

Other Ingredients
*mung beans, whole,
1 cup dry
vegetable oil, 1½ TBS
coconut, unsweetened, 1 TBS
salt, ½ tsp*

Spices
*hing, pinch
seeds mixture, ½ tsp
dried hot pepper, 1
Indian bay leaves, 3
cumin/coriander powder,
1½ tsp
turmeric, ¼ tsp
garam masala, ¼ tsp
Pav Bahji masala, ¼ tsp
(optional: hot red pepper
powder, ¼ tsp)*

To sprout red or green mung beans, soak in warm water in a warm place for 1-2 days:
> **1 cup whole mung beans**

This makes more than the 2 cups of short sprouts needed for this recipe

Heat in a medium saucepan:
> **1½ Tablespoons vegetable oil**
> **pinch hing**

Add, heat and stir for two minutes:
> **½ teaspoon cumin/mustard/sesame seed mixture**
> **1 dried hot pepper**
> **3 Indian bay leaves**
> **1 medium onion, chopped**

Add and stir over medium heat:
> **1½ teaspoons coriander/cumin powder**
> **½ teaspoon salt**
> **¼ teaspoon turmeric**
> **¼ teaspoon garam masala**
> **¼ teaspoon Pav Bahji masala**
> **¼ teaspoon hot pepper powder (opt.)**
> **2 cups mung bean sprouts**
> **¼ cup water**

Stir in after the water has been absorbed:
> **1 Tablespoon unsweetened coconut**

Cover and cook about 10 minutes, stirring occasionally, until the beans are soft. You may need to add more water while cooking to keep them from sticking. You can also add

2 Tablespoons fresh, chopped coriander leaves (cilantro), chopped tomato, and amchur powder and/or lemon juice (just before serving)

YELLOW SPLIT PEA VEGETABLE

YELLOW SPLIT PEAS WITH GINGER, GARLIC, AND SPICES

Soak for one hour (preferably 6 hours or overnight); drain, and grind coarsely:

> ¾ cup dry yellow split peas

Mix in a bowl:

> **the ground split peas (about 1½ cups)**
> **1-2 teaspoons salt**
> **½ jalapeño pepper, ground**
> **½ clove garlic, ground**
> **pinch cumin seeds**
> **¼ inch cube ginger, grated**
> **2 Tablespoons fresh coriander leaves (cilantro),**
> **chopped**

Heat in a saucepan:

> **1½ Tablespoons vegetable oil**
> **pinch hing**
> **½ teaspoon cumin/mustard/sesame seed mixture**

When the seeds pop, add:

> **¾ teaspoon cumin/coriander powder**
> **½ teaspoon turmeric**
> **½ teaspoon sugar**
> **pinch hot red pepper powder (opt.)**
> **the split pea mixture**
> **¼-½ cup water**
> **2 Tablespoons lemon juice**

Cover and simmer about 10 minutes on *very low heat*, stirring occasionally.

Makes 1¾ cups
(traditional serving = 2 TBS)

Per serving: Calories: 38, Protein: 2 gm., Fat: 1.4 gm., Carbohydrates: 5 gm.

• • • •

Fresh Ingredients
jalapeño pepper, ½
garlic, ½ clove
ginger, ¼ inch cube
coriander leaves (cilantro),
  2 TBS
lemon juice, 2 TSP

Other Ingredients
yellow split peas, ¾ cup dry
salt, 1-2 tsp
vegetable oil, 1½ TBS
sugar, ½ tsp

Spices
cumin seeds, pinch
hing, pinch
seeds mixture, ½ tsp
cumin/coriander powder,
  ¾ tsp
turmeric, ½ tsp
(optional: hot red pepper
  powder, pinch)

YOGURT DUMPLINGS

Dumplings of Urad Dal In Yogurt Sauce

Makes about 2 dozen
(traditional serving = 2-3)

*Per serving: Calories: 64,
Protein: 4 gm., Fat: 0.9 gm.,
Carbohydrates: 10 gm.*

• • • •

Fresh Ingredients
*garlic, 1 clove
long hot green pepper, 1
coriander leaves (cilantro),
    2 TBS or more
yogurt, plain, 1 cup
apple butter chutney (see
    recipe)
onion, to taste*

Other Ingredients
*urad dal, 2 cups dry
baking soda, ¼ tsp
salt, 1 TBS + ¼ tsp
(optional: chunks unsweet-
    ened coconut)
vegetable oil for deep frying*
                    (cont.)

Soak in warm water for about 2 hours, then drain:
> **2 cups "black" urad dal**

Grind together in the blender until fine:
> **the soaked dal**
> **1 clove garlic, diced**
> **1 fresh, hot green pepper, chopped**
> **2 Tablespoons fresh coriander leaves (cilantro),
> chopped**
> **1 Tablespoon cumin seeds**
> **1 Tablespoon salt**
> **¼ teaspoon baking soda**

Knead with wet hands. Form into walnut-sized balls, and flatten slightly in your palm. (You may put a small chunk of coconut inside each dumpling at this point.) Cook the dumplings in oil in a deep fryer until browned, then soak them in hot water while making the yogurt mixture below.

Combine in a bowl:
> **1 cup plain yogurt**
> **¼ teaspoon salt**
> **¼ teaspoon ground black pepper**
> **about ½ cup cold water**

Remove the dumplings from the water, press between your palms to squeeze out most of the water, and place in the yogurt mixture.

Make individual servings of several dumplings and yogurt in small bowls, with *all* of the following layered on top:

Apple Butter Chutney, pg. 36 (or a tamarind
    chutney, pgs. 46-7), a liberal amount
raw onion, diced
fresh coriander leaves (cilantro), chopped
hot red pepper powder, to taste
pinch cumin powder
ground black pepper (opt. to taste)

Spices
cumin seeds, 1 TBS
black pepper, ¼ tsp and for
    garnish
hot red pepper powder, to
    taste
cumin powder, pinch

You can also use these dumplings, made slightly larger and
with a hole through the center (like a doughnut), as an
addition to lentil soup. There's no need to soak these in
water if you're using them in soup. You can also freeze the
dumplings *without* the yogurt sauce.

VEGETABLES

BHARTA
Mashed Eggplant with Peanuts and Spices

Simmer in water about 8 minutes, until very soft:
> **1 medium unpeeled eggplant, chopped in large chunks (about 5 cups)**

Drain off the water and mash the eggplant in a bowl.

Add:
> **2 Tablespoons crushed roasted peanuts**
> **2 Tablespoons fresh coriander leaves (cilantro), chopped**

In a saucepan, heat:
> **1½ Tablespoons vegetable oil**
> **pinch hing**
> **1 teaspoon cumin/mustard/sesame seed mixture**

When the seeds pop, add to the saucepan:
> **3 Tablespoons onion, chopped**
> **¼ jalapeño pepper, ground**
> **½ small clove garlic, ground**
> **¼ inch cube fresh ginger, grated**
> **1½ teaspoons coriander/cumin powder**
> **½ teaspoon salt**
> **¼ teaspoon garam masala**
> **¼ teaspoon hot red pepper powder (opt.)**
> **⅛ teaspoon turmeric**
> **pinch cumin seeds**

Sauté until the onions are lightly browned.

Add the eggplant mixture to the saucepan; combine, remove from the heat, and serve.

Makes 1¾ cups
(traditional serving = 2 TBS)

Per serving: Calories: 30, Protein: 0 gm., Fat: 1.9 gm., Carbohydrates: 3 gm.

• • • •

Fresh Ingredients
eggplant, 1 medium
coriander leaves (cilantro), 2 TBS
onion, 3 TBS
jalapeño pepper, ¼
garlic, ½ small clove
ginger, ¼ inch cube

Other Ingredients
peanuts, roasted, 2 TBS
vegetable oil, 1½ TBS
salt, ½ tsp

Spices
hing, pinch
seeds mixture, 1 tsp
cumin/coriander powder, 1½ tsp
garam masala, ¼ tsp
(optional: hot red pepper powder, ¼ tsp)
turmeric, ⅛ tsp
cumin seeds, pinch

BRUSSELS SPROUTS
SPICED BRUSSELS SPROUTS

Wash, trim, and slice:
> **½ lb. fresh Brussels sprouts**

In a small saucepan, heat:
> **½ Tablespoon vegetable oil**
> **1 Tablespoon butter**

Add:
> **pinch hing**
> **½ teaspoon seeds mixture**
> **½ teaspoon cumin seeds**

When the seeds pop, add and sauté till soft:
> **½ medium onion, chopped**
> **½ medium tomato, chopped**

Add:
> **1 Tablespoon fresh coriander leaves (cilantro),**
>   **chopped**
> **1 inch fresh hot green pepper, chopped**
> **1 teaspoon garam masala**
> **½ teaspoon Pav Bahji masala**
> **1 Tablespoon cumin/coriander powder**
> **½-1 teaspoon hot red pepper powder**
> **½ teaspoon turmeric**
> **1 teaspoon salt**

Add:
> **the sliced Brussels sprouts**
> **¼ cup water**

Cover and simmer about 10-15 minutes until the sprouts are soft. Add only a little extra water as it cooks, if necessary, to keep from sticking.

This is one dish which seems less tasty when the butter and oil are much reduced.

Makes 1½ cups
(traditional serving = 2 TBS)

Per serving: Calories: 25,
Protein: 0 gm., Fat: 1.6 gm.,
Carbohydrates: 2 gm.

• • • •

Fresh Ingredients
fresh Brussels sprouts, ½ lb
butter 1 TBS
onion, ½
tomato, ½
coriander leaves (cilantro),
  1 TBS
long hot pepper, 1 inch

Other Ingredients
vegetable oil, ½ TBS
salt, 1 tsp

Spices
hing, pinch
seeds mixture, ½ tsp
cumin seeds, ½ tsp
garam masala, 1 tsp
Pav Bahji masala, ½ tsp
cumin/coriander powder,
  1 TBS
hot red pepper powder,
  ½-1 tsp
turmeric powder, ½ tsp

BUTTERNUT SQUASH

SIMPLE SWEET AND SAVORY BUTTERNUT SQUASH

Makes about 2 cups
(traditional serving = 2 TBS)

*Per serving: Calories: 19,
Protein: 0 gm., Fat: 1.2 gm.,
Carbohydrates: 2 gm.*

• • • •

Fresh Ingredients
butternut squash, ½ lb
butter, unsalted, ½ TBS

Other Ingredients
vegetable oil, 1 TBS
sugar, ½-¾ tsp
salt, ½ tsp

Spices
hing, tiny pinch
seeds mixture, ½ TBS
cumin/coriander powder,
*   ½ tsp*
turmeric, pinch
hot red pepper powder, pinch
*   or to taste*

Peel and chop in small cubes (¼-½ inch):
> **1 (½ lb.) butternut squash (makes about 1½-2 cups
> chopped)**

In a saucepan, heat:
> **1 Tablespoon vegetable oil**
> **tiny pinch hing**
> **½ Tablespoon cumin/mustard/sesame seed
> mixture**

When seeds pop, add the dry spices:
> **½-¾ teaspoon sugar**
> **½ teaspoon cumin/coriander powder**
> **½ teaspoon salt**
> **pinch turmeric**
> **pinch hot red pepper powder, or to taste**

Now add:
> **the cubed squash**
> **½ Tablespoon unsalted butter**
> **2 Tablespoons water**

Cover, turn heat to medium-low, and cook for about 2-5
minutes until squash is soft but not mushy.

CABBAGE WADA CURRY

Spiced Cabbage and Chickpea Flour Dumplings

In a bowl, mix by hand:

    1 cup (packed) cabbage, shredded
    ⅞ cup chickpea flour
    1 Tablespoon fresh coriander leaves (cilantro), chopped
    2 teaspoons cumin/coriander powder
    1 teaspoon salt
    ½ teaspoon turmeric powder
    ½-1 teaspoon hot red pepper powder (opt.)
    ¼ teaspoon garam masala
    pinch hing

Add water, little by little (about ¼ cup total), until the mixture is a sticky paste. Form the paste into walnut-sized balls. Cook in a pressure cooker at medium pressure for about 20 minutes, or steam for 30-40 minutes, until a toothpick inserted in the wada comes out fairly clean.

Deep-fry the balls in very hot oil until brown, and set aside.

In a frying pan or saucepan, heat:

    1 Tablespoon vegetable oil
    pinch hing
    ½ teaspoon cumin/mustard/sesame seed mixture

When seeds pop, add:

    2 Tablespoons fresh coriander leaves (cilantro), chopped
    1 clove garlic, minced
    4 scallions, diced

(cont.)

Makes 16
(traditional serving = 2)

Per serving: Calories: 26, Protein: 1 gm., Fat: 1 gm., Carbohydrates: 3 gm.

• • • •

Fresh Ingredients
cabbage, 1 cup
coriander leaves (cilantro), 3 TBS
garlic, 1 clove
scallions, 4
fresh hot green pepper, 1 TBS
onion, 2 TBS

Other Ingredients
chickpea flour, ⅞ cup
salt, 1½ tsp
vegetable oil, 1 TBS and for deep frying

Spices
cumin/coriander powder, 1 TBS plus 2 tsp
turmeric, 1 tsp
(optional: hot red pepper powder, ½-1½ tsp)
garam masala, ¾ tsp
hing, 2 pinches
seeds mixture, ½ tsp

1 Tablespoon fresh hot pepper, diced
2 Tablespoons onion, chopped
1 Tablespoon cumin/coriander powder
½ teaspoon turmeric
½ teaspoon hot red pepper powder
½ teaspoon garam masala
½ teaspoon salt

Sauté until the scallions and onion are soft, then add the wada balls. Mix well, and serve.

COOKED CABBAGE

SAVORY SHREDDED CABBAGE

Makes 2 cups
(traditional serving = 2 TBS)

Per serving: Calories: 25, Protein: 0 gm., Fat: 1.2 gm., Carbohydrates: 3 gm.

• • • •

Fresh Ingredients
onion, ½ cup
coriander leaves (cilantro), 2 TBS
cabbage, 4 cups raw

Other Ingredients
vegetable oil, 1½ TBS
salt, 1 tsp

Spices
hing, pinch
seeds mixture, 1 tsp
cumin/coriander powder, 2 tsp
hot red pepper powder, ¾-1½ tsp
turmeric powder, 1 tsp
garam masala, ½ tsp

In a large saucepan, heat:
1½ Tablespoons vegetable oil
pinch hing
1 teaspoon cumin/mustard/sesame seed mixture

When the seeds pop, add and sauté until the onion is soft:
½ cup onion, chopped
2 Tablespoons fresh coriander leaves (cilantro), chopped

Add:
2 teaspoons cumin/coriander powder
¾-1½ teaspoons hot red pepper powder
1 teaspoon turmeric
1 teaspoon salt
½ teaspoon garam masala
4 cups raw cabbage, shredded
more water, as needed, to keep the mixture from sticking

Cover and simmer over low heat about 10-15 minutes, until the cabbage is only slightly crunchy.

CORN KACHURI VEGETABLE

Spiced Corn Kernels

Grind together coarsely in a food mill or food processor:

　　　raw (or cooked) kernels from 2 ears of mature corn
　　　1 Tablespoon fresh coriander leaves (cilantro),
　　　　chopped
　　　½-1 fresh jalapeño pepper, chopped
　　　1 teaspoon salt
　　　1 teaspoon cumin seeds

In a saucepan, heat:

　　　2 Tablespoons vegetable oil
　　　pinch hing
　　　½ teaspoon cumin/mustard/sesame seed mixture

When the seeds pop, add:

　　　¼-½ teaspoon cumin/coriander powder
　　　¼ teaspoon turmeric
　　　1 Tablespoon lemon juice

Add the corn mixture and cook over low heat, uncovered, for 10-15 minutes, until dry-ish and lightly browned.

You can substitute frozen corn and still get excellent flavor.

Makes 1¾ cups
(traditional serving = 2 TBS)

Per serving: Calories: 28, Protein: 0 gm., Fat: 0.9 gm., Carbohydrates: 4 gm.

• • • •

Fresh Ingredients
*corn, 2 mature ears, raw
coriander leaves (cilantro),
　1 TBS
jalapeño pepper, ½-1
lemon juice, 1 TBS*

Other Ingredients
*vegetable oil, 2 TBS
salt, 1 tsp*

Spices
*cumin seeds, 1 tsp
hing, pinch
seeds mixture, ½ tsp
cumin/coriander powder,
　¼ -½ tsp
turmeric, ¼ tsp*

Makes 1½ cups
(traditional serving = about 2 TBS)

Per serving: Calories: 21, Protein: 1 gm., Fat: 1.2 gm., Carbohydrates: 2 gm.

• • • •

Fresh Ingredients
coriander leaves (cilantro), 1 TBS

Other Ingredients
vegetable oil, 1 TBS
peanuts, roasted, ¼ cup
canned drumsticks, 1 can*
(optional: lentils, 1 TBS, cooked)

Spices
hing, pinch
seeds mixture, ¼ tsp
cumin/coriander powder, 1 tsp
hot red pepper powder, ¼ tsp or to taste
turmeric, ¼ tsp
garam masala, ¼ teaspoon

DRUMSTICKS
CANNED DRUMSTICK VEGETABLES, LIGHTLY SEASONED

In a saucepan, heat:
>   **1 Tablespoon vegetable oil**
>   **pinch hing**
>   **¼ teaspoon cumin/mustard/sesame seed mixture**

When the seeds pop, add:
>   **1 Tablespoon fresh coriander leaves (cilantro), chopped**
>   **¼ cup roasted peanuts, crushed**
>   **1 teaspoon cumin/coriander powder**
>   **¼ teaspoon hot red pepper powder, or to taste**
>   **¼ teaspoon turmeric**
>   **¼ teaspoon garam masala**

Then add:
>   **1 (14 oz.) can drumsticks, drained* + 1 Tablespoon of the liquid from the can**
>   **¼ cup water**
>   **1 Tablespoon soft-cooked lentils (if available)**

Bring to a boil and simmer for a couple of minutes to let the drumsticks heat through. Like artichoke leaves, these are eaten by drawing out the tender inner part between your teeth and discarding the fibrous outer husk.

*Drumsticks are a long, thin Asian vegetable. If you can't find cans of it in Indian food stores, you can substitute 2 cups steamed bamboo shoots, celery, or eggplant in this recipe.

EGGPLANT AND GREEN BEANS

MILDLY SPICED EGGPLANT WITH GREEN BEANS AND TOMATOES

Wash, trim, split, and cut in ½" pieces:
1½ cups fresh green beans

Wash, trim, cube, and set aside in 2 cups water to avoid discoloring:
2 cups eggplant

Heat in a saucepan:
¼ cup vegetable oil
pinch hing
1 teaspoon cumin/mustard/sesame seed mixture
1 teaspoon cumin seeds

When the seeds pop, add and stir for one minute:
2 large cloves garlic, chopped
1½ cups tomato, chopped
1 cup onion, chopped (opt.)

Add and stir:
2 teaspoons cumin/coriander powder
1 teaspoon salt
½ teaspoon turmeric
¼ teaspoon hot red pepper powder, or to taste

Add and stir:
the green bean pieces
the drained eggplant cubes
½ cup water
¾ teaspoon sugar

Cover and simmer for 15 minutes, until the vegetables are tender.

Makes 2 cups
(traditional serving = 2 TBS)

Per serving: Calories: 39, Protein: 0 gm., Fat: 3.2 gm., Carbohydrates: 2 gm.

• • • •

Fresh Ingredients
fresh green beans, 1½ cups
eggplant, 2 cups
garlic, 2 large cloves
tomato, 1½ cups
(optional: onion, 1 cup)

Other Ingredients
vegetable oil, ¼ cup
salt, 1 tsp
sugar, ¾ tsp

Spices
hing, pinch
seeds mixture, 1 tsp
cumin seeds, 1 tsp
cumin/coriander powder,
*   2 tsp*
turmeric, ½ tsp
hot red pepper powder,
*   ¼ tsp or to taste*

EGGPLANT WITH STUFFING

EGGPLANT WITH A SWEET AND SAVORY STUFFING

Makes 3 cups
(traditional serving = ¼ cup)

Per serving: Calories: 66, Protein: 1 gm., Fat: 4.8 gm., Carbohydrates: 4 gm.

• • • •

Fresh Ingredients
Japanese eggplants, 4 small onion, 1 medium garlic, ½ clove hot green pepper, 2 inches yogurt, plain, ¼ cup coriander leaves (cilantro), 2 TBS

Other Ingredients
peanuts, roasted, 2 TBS coconut, unsweetened, 1 TBS salt, ½ tsp vegetable oil, 3 TBS

(cont.)

Wash:

> **4 small, unpeeled Japanese eggplants (regular eggplants will be too seedy)**

Slice ¾"-1" thick, then score each slice with an "x" ¾ of the way through. Place in a bowl and cover with water to prevent darkening.

In a separate small bowl, mix by hand:

> **1 medium onion, finely diced**
> **½ clove garlic, chopped**
> **2 inches fresh hot green pepper, chopped**
> **¼ cup yogurt**
> **2 Tablespoons roasted peanuts, chopped very finely**
> **1 Tablespoon coconut**
> **1 teaspoon cumin/coriander powder**
> **1 teaspoon garam masala,**
> **or ½ tsp each garam masala and another masala**
> **½-1 teaspoon hot red pepper powder (opt.)**
> **½ teaspoon turmeric**
> **½ teaspoon salt**
> **2 Tablespoons fresh coriander leaves (cilantro), chopped**

Drain the eggplant slices. Stuff this mixture into the score lines in the slices, and set aside in a bowl with any remaining stuffing.

Heat in a saucepan:

3 Tablespoons vegetable oil
pinch of hing
½ teaspoon cumin/mustard/sesame seeds
1-2 Indian bay leaves
1 dried hot pepper

When the seeds pop, carefully add the eggplant, stuffed side up, and sauté for several minutes.

Add:

¼-½ cup water

Cover and cook over low heat, gently stirring occasionally, until eggplant is soft (about 10 minutes).

This can also be cooked in the microwave. Just assemble all the ingredients in a microwavable dish, add ¼ cup water, cover, and cook on full power for about 10 minutes, until the eggplant is soft.

Spices
cumin/coriander powder,
* 1 tsp*
garam masala, 1 tsp
(optional: hot red pepper
* powder, ½-1 tsp)*
turmeric, ½ tsp
hing, pinch
seeds mixture, ½ tsp
Indian bay leaves, 1-2
dried hot pepper, 1

GREEN PEPPERS WITH STUFFING

GREEN PEPPERS WITH CHICKPEA FLOUR STUFFING

Makes 4 peppers
(traditional serving =
¼-½ pepper)

Per serving: Calories: 134,
Protein: 1 gm., Fat: 11.2 gm.,
Carbohydrates: 6 gm.

• • • •

Fresh Ingredients
sweet green peppers, 4
coriander leaves (cilantro),
1 TBS

Other Ingredients
chickpea flour, 1 cup
vegetable oil, ⅔ cup
salt, 1 tsp
sugar, ¼ tsp

Spices
cumin/coriander, 1 TBS
turmeric, ½ tsp
hot red pepper powder,
¼ tsp or to taste
hing, pinch
seeds mixture, 1 tsp

Slice off the tops of:
4 sweet green peppers

Trim the tops, remove the seeds, and set the peppers aside.

In a bowl, mix thoroughly by hand:
1 cup chickpea flour
1 Tablespoon fresh coriander leaves (cilantro), chopped
⅓ cup vegetable oil
1 Tablespoon cumin/coriander powder
1 teaspoon salt
½ teaspoon turmeric
¼ teaspoon hot red pepper powder, or to taste
¼ teaspoon sugar
¼ cup water

Stuff this mixture into each of the peppers (it need not fill the pepper to the top), and replace the tops.

Heat in a saucepan:
⅓ cup vegetable oil
pinch hing
1 teaspoon cumin/mustard/sesame seed mixture

When the seeds pop, add the stuffed green peppers, and reduce the heat to low. Cover and cook, turning the peppers about every 5 minutes, until well browned (usually about 20 minutes). Cut the peppers into quarters, and serve.

The texture and consistency of this dish suffers if the amount of oil is reduced.

INDIAN CUCUMBERS
SMALL INDIAN CUCUMBERS, LIGHTLY SEASONED

In a small saucepan, heat:
> **1 Tablespoon vegetable oil**
> **pinch hing**
> **½ teaspoon black mustard seeds**

When the seeds pop, add:
> **1 clove garlic, chopped**
> **1 Tablespoon fresh coriander leaves (cilantro), chopped**
> **1 teaspoon cumin/coriander powder**
> **½ teaspoon turmeric powder**
> **¼-½ teaspoon hot red pepper powder**
> **¼ teaspoon salt**
> **15 small Indian cucumbers (tandoora)*, in ¼" slices (about 2 cups)**

Cover and sauté over low heat about 15-20 minutes, until the cucumbers are soft. Do not add water.

Serve sprinkled with more salt to taste, if desired.

*Indian cucumbers are about 2½" long and 1" across, sometimes reddish inside. Do not substitute salad or pickling cucumbers in this recipe; you will not get the same results!

Makes 1-1½ cups
(traditional serving = 2 TBS)

Per serving: Calories: 12, Protein: 0 gm., Fat: 1 gm., Carbohydrates: 1 gm.

• • • •

Fresh Ingredients
garlic, 1 clove
coriander leaves (cilantro), 1 TBS
Indian cucumbers (tandoora), 15

Other Ingredients
vegetable oil, 1 TBS
salt, ¼ tsp

Spices
hing, pinch
black mustard seeds, ½ tsp
cumin/coriander powder, 1 tsp
turmeric powder, ½ tsp
hot red pepper powder, ¼-½ tsp

INDIAN GREEN BEANS

Flat Indian Green Beans with Peanuts and Spices

Makes 2 cups
(traditional serving = 2 TBS)

Per serving: Calories: 35, Protein: 1 gm., Fat: 2.6 gm., Carbohydrates: 2 gm.

••••

Fresh Ingredients
Indian green beans, 3 cups
coriander leaves (cilantro),
2 TBS*

Other Ingredients
*peanuts, roasted, ¼ cup
vegetable oil, 2 TBS
(optional: tamarind paste,
½ tsp)
salt, 2 tsp*

Spices
*hing, pinch
seeds mixture, ½ tsp
cumin/coriander powder,
2 tsp
turmeric, ½ tsp
hot red pepper powder,
1-1½ tsp*

In a small bowl, combine:
> **3 cups Indian green beans*, trimmed and chopped into 1-inch pieces**
> **2 cups water**
> **¼ cup roasted peanuts, crushed**

In a saucepan, heat:
> **2 Tablespoons vegetable oil**
> **pinch hing**
> **½ teaspoon cumin/mustard/sesame seed mixture**

When the seeds pop, add:
> **2 Tablespoons fresh coriander leaves (cilantro), chopped**
> **2 teaspoons cumin/coriander powder**
> **2 teaspoons salt**
> **½ teaspoon turmeric**
> **1-1½ teaspoon hot red pepper powder, or to taste**
> **½ teaspoon tamarind paste (opt.)**

Add the bean mixture and simmer vigorously, uncovered, for about 20 minutes, adding more water as necessary to prevent sticking.

*Do not substitute snap beans; they are too tender for this kind of vigorous boiling. You can use pole beans, but cook for only 10 minutes.

INDIAN ZUCCHINI
SPINY INDIAN ZUCCHINI, LIGHTLY SPICED

Remove the spines from and slice into ½ circles:

> **2 cups Indian zucchini* (save spines for *Zucchini Spine Chutney*, pg. 49)**

In a small saucepan, heat:

> **1 Tablespoon vegetable oil**
> **tiny pinch of hing**
> **1 teaspoon cumin/mustard/sesame seed mixture**

When the seeds pop, add:

> **1½ teaspoons cumin/coriander powder**
> **½-1 teaspoon hot red pepper powder**
> **½ teaspoon salt**
> **¼ teaspoon garam masala**
> **¼ teaspoon turmeric**
> **1½ Tablespoons roasted peanuts, chopped**
> **the sliced zucchini**
> **about ¼ cup water**

Cover and simmer until the zucchini is soft.

*If you don't have Indian zucchini, you can substitute regular zucchini. Indian zucchini have thin ridges running lengthwise down the peel. Though called "spines," these ridges are not sharp; you can easily peel them off with a vegetable peeler.

Makes 1½ cups
(traditional serving = 2 TBS)

Per serving: Calories: 20, Protein: 0 gm., Fat: 1.6 gm., Carbohydrates: 1 gm.

• • • •

Fresh Ingredients
Indian zucchini,* 2 cups

Other Ingredients
vegetable oil, 1 TBS
peanuts, roasted, 1½ TBS
salt, ½ tsp

Spices
hing, tiny pinch
seeds mixture, 1 tsp
cumin/coriander powder,
*   1½ tsp*
hot red pepper powder,
*   ½-1 tsp*
garam masala, ¼ tsp
turmeric, ¼ tsp

MIXED VEGETABLES
SEASONED POTATOES, CAULIFLOWER, RED PEPPERS, AND TOMATOES WITH COCONUT

Makes 2½ cups
(traditional serving = 2 TBS)

*Per serving: Calories: 18,
Protein: 0 gm., Fat: 0.9 gm.,
Carbohydrates: 2 gm.*

• • • •

Fresh Ingredients
*onion, ½ cup
tomato, 1 small
coriander leaves (cilantro),
 1 TBS
potato, 1 medium
cauliflower, ½ cup
sweet red peppers, ½ cup*

Other Ingredients
*vegetable oil, 1 TBS
canned crushed tomatoes,
 ¼ cup
coconut, unsweetened, ½ TBS
salt, ½ tsp*

Spices
*hing, pinch
seeds mixture, ½ tsp
cumin/coriander powder, 1 tsp
garam masala, ½ tsp
(optional: roasted cumin
 seeds, ½ tsp)
hot red pepper powder, ¼-½ tsp
turmeric, ¼ tsp
Pav Bahji masala, ¼ tsp*

In a large saucepan, heat:
> **1 Tablespoon vegetable oil**
> **pinch hing**
> **½ teaspoon cumin/mustard/sesame seed mixture**

When the seeds pop, add and sauté until the onion is soft:
> **½ cup onion, chopped**
> **1 small tomato, chopped**
> **¼ cup canned crushed tomatoes**

Add:
> **1 Tablespoon fresh coriander leaves (cilantro), chopped**
> **1 teaspoon cumin/coriander powder**
> **½ teaspoon salt**
> **½ teaspoon garam masala**
> **½ teaspoon roasted cumin seeds (opt.)**
> **¼-½ teaspoon hot red pepper powder**
> **¼ teaspoon turmeric**
> **¼ teaspoon Pav Bahji masala**

Add:
> **1 medium raw potato, chopped small**
> **½ cup raw cauliflower, chopped small**
> **½ cup raw red sweet pepper, chopped small**
> **½ Tablespoon coconut**
> **½ cup water**

You may add other vegetables too, like carrots, eggplant, red potatoes with the skin on, etc. Cover and let simmer over low heat for about 5-10 minutes, until the vegetables are softened but still a little crunchy.

OKRA WITH PEANUT STUFFING

SMALL OKRA DRY-COOKED WITH SPICY PEANUT STUFFING

In a bowl, combine:
> 2 Tablespoons roasted peanuts, crushed
> 1 Tablespoon coriander leaves (cilantro), chopped
> 1-2 teaspoons shredded, unsweetened coconut
> 1 teaspoon vegetable oil
> 1 teaspoon amchur powder
> 1 teaspoon cumin/coriander powder
> ½-1 teaspoon hot red pepper powder
> ½ teaspoon salt
> ½ teaspoon turmeric

Stuff this mixture into:
> 2 cups of 2" okra, ends trimmed off, and
> split down one side

In a small saucepan, heat:
> 2 Tablespoons vegetable oil
> pinch hing
> ½ teaspoon seeds mixture

When the seeds pop, add and sauté the stuffed okra. (It is OK to heap them in the pan). When all the okra are in, toss them, cover, and cook over a low flame about 20-30 minutes, until soft. Periodically, wipe the condensed water off the lid (to prevent the okra from becoming slimy), and toss again.

Makes 1½ cups
(traditional serving = 2 TBS)

Per serving: Calories: 19,
Protein: 1 gm., Fat: 1 gm.,
Carbohydrates: 2 gm.

• • • •

Fresh Ingredients
coriander leaves (cilantro),
* 1 TBS, chopped*
okra, 2 cups, trimmed and
* slit*

Other Ingredients
roasted peanuts, 2 TBS,
* crushed*
unsweetened coconut,
* 1-2 tsp*
vegetable oil, 2 TBS + 1 tsp
salt, 1½ tsp

Spices
amchur powder, 1 tsp
cumin/coriander powder,
* 1 tsp*
hot red pepper powder,
* ½-1 tsp*
turmeric, ½ tsp
hing, pinch
seeds mixture, ½ tsp

Makes 1½ cups
(traditional serving = 2 TBS)

Per serving: Calories: 13,
Protein: 0 gm., Fat: 1 gm.,
Carbohydrates: 1 gm.

• • • •

Fresh Ingredients
onion, ¼ cup, chopped
tomato, ¼ cup chopped
coriander leaves (cilantro),
* 1 TBS, chopped*
hot pepper mixture, 1 tsp
* (see pg. 102)*
garlic, to taste
okra, 1 cup, chopped

Other Ingredients
vegetable oil, 1 TBS
salt, ¼ tsp

Spices
hing, pinch
seeds mixture, ¼ tsp
cumin/coriander powder,
* 1 tsp*
hot red pepper powder,
* ¼-½ tsp*
turmeric, ¼ tsp

OKRA VEGETABLE
CHOPPED OKRA STEWED WITH VEGETABLES AND SPICES

In a small saucepan, heat:
> **1 Tablespoon vegetable oil**
> **pinch hing**
> **¼ teaspoon cumin/mustard/sesame seed mixture**

When the seeds pop, add and sauté:
> **¼ cup onion, chopped**
> **¼ cup tomato, chopped**
> **1 Tablespoon coriander leaves (cilantro), chopped**
> **1 teaspoon hot pepper mixture (see recipe for**
> **   *Black-Eyed Pea Curry*, pg. 102)**
> **garlic to taste**

When these vegetables are very soft, add:
> **1 teaspoon cumin/coriander powder**
> **¼-½ teaspoon hot red pepper powder**
> **¼ teaspoon turmeric**
> **¼ teaspoon salt**
> **1 cup okra, chopped**

Cover and cook on low heat until the okra is soft.

ONION VEGETABLE

CHOPPED ONIONS WITH PEANUTS AND SPICES

In a bowl, combine:
> **3 cups onion, chopped**
> **2½ Tablespoons roasted peanuts, chopped**
> **1½ Tablespoons coriander leaves (cilantro), chopped**
> **1½ teaspoons cumin/coriander powder**
> **¾ teaspoon salt**
> **½-¾ teaspoon hot red pepper powder**
> **¼ teaspoon garam masala**

In a saucepan, heat:
> **1 Tablespoon vegetable oil**
> **pinch of hing**
> **¾ teaspoon cumin/mustard/sesame seed mixture**
> **3-4 Indian bay leaves**
> **1 whole dried hot pepper**

When seeds pop, add:
> **¾ teaspoon turmeric**
> **the onion mixture**
> **1½ Tablespoons water**

Turn the heat to low, cover tightly, and simmer for 10 minutes. The onions should still be a little crunchy.

You can use Bermuda onion for extra sweetness and color, but the leftovers won't keep quite as well.

Makes 1¾ cups
(traditional serving = 2 TBS)

Per serving: Calories: 30, Protein: 1 gm., Fat: 1.7 gm., Carbohydrates: 3 gm.

• • • •

Fresh Ingredients
onion, 3 cups
coriander leaves (cilantro), 1½ TBS

Other Ingredients
peanuts, roasted, 2½ TBS
vegetable oil, 1 TBS
salt, ¾ tsp

Spices
cumin/coriander powder, 1½ tsp
hot red pepper powder, ½-¾ tsp
garam masala, ¼ tsp
hing, pinch
seeds mixture, ¾ tsp
Indian bay leaves, 3-4
dried hot pepper, 1 whole
turmeric, ¾ tsp

ONIONS WITH STUFFING

SMALL BOILING ONIONS WITH PEANUT AND COCONUT STUFFING

Makes 20 onions
(traditional serving = 2)

Per serving: Calories: 232,
Protein: 4 gm., Fat: 18.6 gm.,
Carbohydrates: 11 gm.

● ● ● ●

Fresh Ingredients
boiling onions, 20 small
coriander leaves (cilantro),
*   ¼ cup*
garlic, ½ clove

Other Ingredients
coconut, unsweetened, 1 cup
peanuts, roasted, ½ cup
vegetable oil, 1 TBS + 1 tsp
salt, 2 tsp

Spices
cumin/coriander powder,
*   2 TBS*
turmeric, 1½ tsp
hot red pepper powder,
*   ½-1 tsp*
garam masala, ½ tsp
hing, pinch
seeds mixture, 1 tsp

Peel and score with an "x" half-way through:
> **20 (1"-1½") boiling onions**

In a small bowl, combine:
> **1 cup unsweetened, shredded coconut**
> **½ cup roasted peanuts, crushed**
> **¼ cup fresh coriander leaves (cilantro), chopped**
> **½ clove garlic, diced**
> **2 Tablespoons cumin/coriander powder**
> **2 teaspoons salt**
> **1 teaspoon turmeric**
> **½-1 teaspoon hot red pepper powder**
> **½ teaspoon garam masala**
> **1 teaspoon vegetable oil**

Press this mixture into the onions.

Heat in a saucepan:
> **1 Tablespoon oil**
> **pinch hing**
> **1 teaspoon cumin/mustard/sesame seed mixture**

When the seeds pop, add:
> **½ teaspoon turmeric**
> **the onions and any loose stuffing left over**
> **½-1 cup water**

Cover and simmer for 10 minutes until the onions are cooked but still slightly crunchy.

PATRA
Seasoned Chickpea and Vegetable Roll

Slice up into ¼" cubes:
1 (12½ oz.) can prepared patra*

In a small frying pan, heat:
2 Tablespoons vegetable oil
pinch hing
1 teaspoon sesame seeds
½ teaspoon cumin/mustard/sesame seed mixture

When the seeds pop, add the patra, toss, and sauté until warmed through.

*Patra is a curried vegetable dish made of arvi leaves stuffed and rolled with a spiced wheat and chickpea flour mixture.

Makes 2 cups
(traditional serving = 2 TBS)

Per serving: Calories: 55, Protein: 1 gm., Fat: 2 gm., Carbohydrates: 7 gm.

• • • •

Fresh Ingredients

Other Ingredients
patra, one can
vegetable oil, 2 TBS
sesame seeds, 1 tsp

Spices
hing, pinch
seeds mixture, ½ tsp

PEAS (MUTTER) PANEER
Seasoned Peas with Ricotta Squares

To make the paneer, spread in an 8" buttered baking pan:
1 pound ricotta cheese

Cook, uncovered, at 350° for 1-2 hours until it is firm and very slightly browned on top. Cut into 1" x ½" squares, and drain on paper towels, pressing lightly. Deep fry the squares in a basket, and drain off the oil. Set aside the paneer. The deep frying can be skipped, if desired. The unfried paneer will taste a little different, will not hold together quite as

Makes 3 ¾ cups
(traditional serving = 2 TBS)

Per serving: Calories: 29, Protein: 1 gm., Fat: 1.4 gm., Carbohydrates: 2 gm.
(cont.)

Fresh Ingredients
ricotta cheese, 1 pound
tomato, 1 medium
onion, 1 medium
coriander leaves (cilantro),
  2 TBS
garlic, 1 clove
peas, 1 (10 oz.) package,
  frozen
(optional: sour cream or
  yogurt, 1 TBS)

Other Ingredients
vegetable oil, 1 TBS
tomato paste, 2 TBS
salt, 1½ tsp

Spices
cloves, 4-5 whole
black peppercorns, 4-5 whole
cinnamon stick, 1-2 inches
hing, pinch
seeds mixture, 1 tsp
Indian bay leaves, 1 TBS
cumin/coriander powder,
  2 tsp
garam masala, 2 tsp
turmeric, 1 tsp
hot red pepper powder,
  ¾-1½ tsp

well, and will soak up the sauce more. Since you will only need part of the paneer for this recipe, you can freeze the remaining amount in an airtight container for later use.

Roast in a dry pan over a medium flame until browned (about 8 minutes), then grind together:

> **4-5 whole cloves**
> **4-5 whole black peppers**
> **1-2 inches cinnamon stick, broken up**

Heat in a saucepan:

> **1 Tablespoon vegetable oil**
> **pinch of hing**
> **1 teaspoon cumin/mustard/sesame seed mix**

When the seeds pop, add and sauté for a few minutes:

> **1 medium tomato, chopped finely**
> **1 medium onion, chopped finely**
> **2 Tablespoons fresh coriander leaves (cilantro), chopped**
> **1 clove garlic, chopped finely**

Add the following dry spices:

> **1 Tablespoon Indian bay leaves, crumbled**
> **2 teaspoons cumin/coriander powder**
> **2 teaspoons garam masala**
> **1 teaspoon turmeric**
> **¾-1½ teaspoons hot red pepper powder**

Add:

> **the roasted, ground cloves, peppercorns, and cinnamon stick**

Add and simmer until the peas are cooked:

> **2 Tablespoons tomato paste**
> **1½ teaspoons salt**
> **1 (10 oz.) package frozen peas**
> **about ¾ cup water**

Stir in and serve:

> **⅓-½ of the prepared paneer**
> **1 Tablespoon sour cream or yogurt (opt.)**

POTATO CURRY
POTATOES WITH TOMATO, SPICES, AND COCONUT

Peel and simmer in a small saucepan until soft, then chop:
> **2 medium potatoes**

Mix together:
> **1 tomato, chopped**
> **1 small onion, chopped**
> **½ fresh hot green pepper, chopped**

Heat in a saucepan:
> **2 Tablespoons vegetable oil**
> **tiny pinch hing**
> **¼ teaspoon cumin/mustard/sesame seed mixture**
> **1 dried hot pepper**
> **2 Tablespoons fresh coriander leaves (cilantro), chopped**
> **½ clove garlic, diced**

When the seeds pop, add:
> **the tomato mixture**
> **1 teaspoon cumin/coriander powder**
> **½-1 teaspoon hot red pepper powder (opt.)**
> **½ teaspoon turmeric**
> **½ teaspoon salt**
> **½ teaspoon Pav Bahji masala**

Then add and toss gently:
> **the chopped potatoes**
> **½ teaspoon fresh lemon juice**

Turn off heat and add:
> **more fresh coriander leaves (cilantro)**
> **¼ cup fresh or dry unsweetened coconut**

You can add extra water, if you wish, to make a lovely gravy. To thicken the gravy, crush a few pieces of potato, and mix well.

Makes 2½ cups
(traditional serving = 2 TBS)

Per serving: Calories: 45, Protein: 0 gm., Fat: 3 gm., Carbohydrates: 4 gm.

••••

Fresh Ingredients
potatoes, 2 medium
tomato, 1
onion, 1 small
fresh hot pepper, ½
coriander leaves (cilantro),
* 2 TBS+ to taste*
garlic, ½ clove
lemon juice, ½ tsp

Other Ingredients
vegetable oil, 2 TBS
salt, ½ tsp
coconut, unsweetened, ¼ cup

Spices
hing, tiny pinch
seeds mixture, ¼ tsp
dried hot pepper, 1
cumin/coriander powder, 1 tsp
(optional: hot red pepper
* powder, ½ -1 tsp)*
turmeric, ½ tsp
Pav Bahji masala, ½ tsp

POTATO DHAMALU
SMALL POTATOES IN A SPICY SAUCE

Makes about 4 cups
(traditional serving =
2 potatoes)

Per serving: Calories: 71,
Protein: 3 gm., Fat: 2.4 gm.,
Carbohydrates: 10 gm.

• • • •

Fresh Ingredients
boiling potatoes, 20 (1"-1½")
tomato, 1 cup
onion, 1 cup
coriander leaves (cilantro),
¼ cup
garlic, 2 cloves
ginger, 2 inches

Other Ingredients
vegetable oil, for deep frying
and 1 TBS
Indian poppy seeds, 2 TBS
salt, 2 tsp

Spices
hing, pinch
seeds mixture, 2 tsp
cumin/coriander powder, 4 tsp
turmeric, 2 tsp
garam masala, 2 tsp
hot red pepper powder,
½-1 tsp

Peel, prick all over with a fork, and soak in salted water:
   20 (1"-1½") boiling potatoes

When all the potatoes are prepared, drain on paper towels and pat dry. Deep fry until brown and set aside.

In a saucepan, heat:
   1 Tablespoon vegetable oil
   pinch hing
   2 teaspoons cumin/mustard/sesame seed mixture

When the seeds pop, add:
   1 cup tomato, chopped
   1 cup onion, chopped
   ¼ cup fresh coriander leaves (cilantro), chopped
   2 cloves garlic, minced
   2 inches fresh ginger, grated
   2 Tablespoons Indian poppy seeds,* ground with
      a little water
   4 teaspoons cumin/coriander powder
   2 teaspoons turmeric
   2 teaspoons salt
   2 teaspoons garam masala
   ½-1 teaspoon hot red pepper powder

Sauté over very low heat until the onion is very soft. Add the fried potatoes and ⅓ cup water. Cover and simmer over low heat for about 5 minutes.

*Don't substitute regular poppy seeds for Indian ones; just omit if necessary.

POTATO NO TOMATO
A QUICKER POTATO CURRY

Peel, boil until soft, dice, and set aside:
>   **½ pound potatoes (1½ cups diced)**

In a saucepan, heat:
>   **1 Tablespoon vegetable oil**

Add and sauté until soft:
>   **1 medium onion, chopped**

Add:
>   **½ clove garlic, chopped**
>   **½ teaspoon fresh grated ginger**
>   **¼ teaspoon turmeric**
>   **pinch cumin seeds**
>   **pinch black mustard seeds**
>   **pinch coriander powder**
>   **pinch hot red pepper powder**

Add:
>   **the diced potatoes**
>   **¼ teaspoon lemon juice**
>   **¼ cup dried, shredded unsweetened coconut**
>   **salt to taste**

Makes 1½ cups
(traditional serving = 2 TBS)

Per serving: Calories: 62,
Protein: 1 gm., Fat: 4 gm.,
Carbohydrates: 6 gm.

• • • •

Fresh Ingredients
potatoes, ½ pound
onion, 1 medium
garlic, ½ clove
ginger, ½ tsp
lemon juice, ¼ tsp

Other Ingredients
vegetable oil, 1 TBS
coconut, unsweetened,
   ¼ cup
salt, to taste

Spices
turmeric, ¼ tsp
cumin seeds, pinch
mustard seeds, pinch
coriander powder, pinch
hot red pepper powder, pinch

SPINACH (SAAG) PANEER

Seasoned Spinach with Ricotta Squares

Makes 3 cups
(traditional serving = 2 TBS)

Per serving: Calories: 20, Protein: 1 gm., Fat: 1.2 gm., Carbohydrates: 1 gm.

• • • •

Fresh Ingredients
ricotta cheese, 1 pound
frozen spinach, 1 10-oz package
tomato, ½ cup
onion, ½ cup
jalapeño pepper, ½
garlic, ½ small clove
ginger, 1 inch cube
coriander leaves (cilantro), 1 TBS

Other Ingredients
vegetable oil, 1 TBS (or ghee)
chickpea flour, 1 TBS
salt, 1 tsp

(cont.)

To make the paneer, spread in an 8" buttered baking pan:
>**1 pound ricotta cheese**

Cook, uncovered, at 350° for 1-2 hours until it is firm and very slightly browned on top. Cut into 1" x ½" squares, and drain on paper towels, pressing lightly. Deep fry the squares in a basket, and drain off the oil. Set aside the paneer. The deep frying can be skipped, if desired. The unfried paneer will taste a little different, will not hold together quite as well, and will soak up the sauce more. Since you will only need part of the paneer for this recipe, you can freeze the remaining amount in an airtight container for later use.

Defrost and set aside:
>**1 package (10 oz.) frozen chopped spinach**

In a large saucepan, heat:
>**1 Tablespoon vegetable oil (or ghee)**
>**pinch hing**
>**1 teaspoon cumin seeds**
>**3 Indian bay leaves**

Then add and sauté until the onion is transparent:
>**½ cup tomato, chopped**
>**½ cup onion, chopped**
>**½ jalapeño pepper ground**
>**½ small clove garlic, ground**
>**1 inch fresh ginger, grated**
>**1 Tablespoon coriander leaves (cilantro), chopped**
>**1 Tablespoon cumin/coriander powder**

1 teaspoon garam masala
1 teaspoon turmeric
½-1 teaspoon hot red pepper powder (opt.)

Then add:
    the defrosted spinach

Put in a small cup:
    1 Tablespoon chickpea flour

Gradually add ½ cup water to the flour, stirring to keep smooth. Add this mixture to the spinach, and stir. Simmer on low heat for 20-30 minutes, uncovered, adding small amounts of water as needed to keep it from sticking.

Gently add in:
    ¼-½ cup paneer

Heat for 2-3 minutes more, and serve.

Spices
hing, pinch
cumin seeds, 1 tsp
Indian bay leaves, 3
cumin/coriander powder,
  1 TBS
garam masala, 1 tsp
turmeric, 1 tsp
(optional: hot red pepper
  powder, ½-1 tsp)

TOMATO VEGETABLE

Chopped Tomatoes Seasoned with Peanuts and Spices

Makes 1½ cups
(traditional serving = 2 TBS)

*Per serving: Calories: 42,
Protein: 1 gm., Fat: 2.9 gm.,
Carbohydrates: 2 gm.*

• • • •

Fresh Ingredients
*tomato, 2 cups
coriander leaves (cilantro),
  2 TBS*

Other Ingredients
*peanuts, roasted, ⅓ cup
salt, ½ tsp
sugar, ½ tsp
vegetable oil, 1 TBS*

Spices
*cumin/coriander powder,
  1½ tsp
hot red pepper powder,
  ¼-½ tsp
turmeric, ¼ tsp
hing, pinch
seeds mixture, ¼ tsp*

Mix together in a bowl:
> **2 cups tomato, chopped**
> **⅓ cup roasted peanuts, crushed**
> **2 Tablespoons fresh coriander leaves (cilantro),
>   chopped**
> **1½ teaspoons cumin/coriander powder**
> **½ teaspoon salt**
> **½ teaspoon sugar**
> **¼-½ teaspoon hot red pepper powder**
> **¼ teaspoon turmeric**

Heat in a saucepan:
> **1 Tablespoon vegetable oil**

Add:
> **tiny pinch hing**
> **¼ teaspoon cumin/mustard/sesame seed mixture**

When the seeds pop, add:
> **the tomato mixture**

Simmer 5-10 minutes without adding extra water.

ZUCCHINI CURRY
Zucchini Seasoned with Spices and Peanuts

Heat in a saucepan:

    1 Tablespoon vegetable oil
    tiny pinch hing
    ¼ tsp. cumin/mustard/sesame seed mixture

When the seeds pop, add:

    2 Tablespoons fresh coriander leaves (cilantro),
        minced
    about 1 teaspoon salt (or to taste)
    ¾ teaspoon cumin/coriander powder
    ½ teaspoon Indian bay leaves
    ¼-½ teaspoon hot red pepper powder
    ¼ teaspoon turmeric
    ¼ teaspoon garam masala
    ¼ teaspoon Pav Bahji masala
    1 dried hot pepper

Then add:

    2 medium zucchini, peeled and chopped (about
        3½ cups)
    1 Tablespoon roasted peanuts, crushed
    ½ cup water

Simmer for about 10 minutes, until the zucchini is soft.

Makes 2¼ cups
(traditional serving = 2 TBS)

*Per serving: Calories: 13,
Protein: 0 gm., Fat: 0.9 gm.,
Carbohydrates: 1 gm.*

• • • •

Fresh Ingredients
*coriander leaves (cilantro),
  2 TBS
zucchini, 2 medium*

Other Ingredients
*vegetable oil, 1 TBS
salt, 1 tsp
peanuts, roasted, 1 TBS*

Spices
*hing, tiny pinch
seeds mixture, ¼ tsp
cumin/coriander powder,
  ¾ tsp
Indian bay leaves, ½ tsp
hot red pepper powder,
  ¼-½ tsp
turmeric, ¼ tsp
garam masala, ¼ tsp
Pav Bahji masala, ¼ tsp
dried hot pepper, 1*

ZUCCHINI KOFTA
ZUCCHINI BALLS IN SAVORY SAUCE

Makes 28
(traditional serving = 2)

*Per serving: Calories: 70,
Protein: 2 gm., Fat: 3.2 gm.,
Carbohydrates: 8 gm.*

• • • •

Fresh Ingredients
*zucchini, 2 medium
coriander leaves (cilantro),
   2½ TBS
onion, 1
tomato, 1
garlic, 1 clove
ginger, ¼ inch cube
fresh hot pepper, a few slices
sour cream (or yogurt) 1 TBS*

Other Ingredients
*chickpea flour, 1½ -2 cups
salt, 2 tsp
vegetable oil, 3 TBS
tomato paste, 1 TBS
vegetable oil for deep-frying*

In a medium bowl, mix:
> 2 medium zucchini, peeled and shredded
> 1½-2 cups chickpea flour, enough to make a
>   thick paste
> 2 Tablespoons fresh coriander leaves (cilantro),
>   chopped
> 1 Tablespoon cumin/coriander powder
> 1 teaspoon salt
> ½-1 teaspoon hot red pepper powder
> ½ teaspoon turmeric
> ½ teaspoon garam masala
> ½ teaspoon oregano seeds (ajama)

Fry the mixture about a tablespoon at a time in deep oil
until browned. Drain and set aside.

Roast in a dry pan until brown, then powder in the blender:
> 4-5 (½") pieces cinnamon stick
> 10 peppercorns
> 4-5 cloves
> ¼ teaspoon cumin seeds

In a large saucepan, heat:
> 3 Tablespoons vegetable oil
> pinch hing
> ½ teaspoon seeds mixture

When seeds pop, add:
> 1 onion, diced
> 1 tomato, diced
> 1 clove garlic, diced
> ½ Tablespoon of coriander leaves (cilantro),
>   chopped
> ¼ inch fresh ginger, grated
> a few slices of fresh hot pepper

½ cup water
1 Tablespoon tomato paste
1 teaspoon cumin/coriander powder
1 teaspoon garam masala
1 teaspoon salt
¼-½ teaspoon hot pepper powder
¼ teaspoon turmeric
the powdered roasted spices (from above)

Cook until the vegetables are soft (about 5 minutes), adding more water as needed.

Then add:
1 Tablespoon sour cream or yogurt
the prepared zucchini balls

Powdered Spices
cumin/coriander, 4 tsp
hot red pepper powder,
*   ½-1½ tsp*
turmeric, ¼ tsp
garam masala, 1½ tsp
hing, pinch

Whole Spices
oregano seeds (ajama), ½ tsp
cinnamon, 4-5 (½") pieces
peppercorns, 10
cloves, 4-5
cumin seeds, ¼ tsp
seeds mix, ½ tsp

DESERTS

ANARASAY

FLAKY, EGG-LESS SUGAR COOKIES WITH COCONUT

Makes 2 dozen
(traditional serving = 1)

*Per serving: Calories: 74,
Protein: 1 gm., Fat: 4.1 gm.,
Carbohydrates: 9 gm.*

Fresh Ingredients

Other Ingredients
*ghee, ½ cup
all-purpose flour, 1 cup
baking soda, ¼ tsp
confectioners' sugar, 1 cup
Indian poppy seeds,* 1-2 tsp
  to top
coconut, unsweetened and
  shredded, 1-2 tsp to top*

Spices

Preheat oven to about 350°.

In a flat pan, rub with fingers to spread:
½ cup liquid ghee

Mix together:
**1 cup white all-purpose flour
¼ teaspoon baking soda**

Add to the ghee alternately, kneading in bit by bit:
**the flour mixture
1 cup confectioners' sugar**

Break off small pieces of dough, and roll into ¾" balls. Press out on an ungreased cookie sheet into thin circles, stars, or other shapes about ¹⁄₁₆" thick and 2½" in diameter.

Sprinkle with and press in:
**1-2 teaspoons Indian poppy seeds*
1-2 teaspoons unsweetened, shredded coconut**

Bake for 5-10 minutes until only *slightly* browned. Let cool and serve.

*If you do not have Indian poppy seeds, do not substitute regular poppy seeds, just omit the seeds altogether. The cookies will still be terrific.

BALU SHAHI
GLAZED SWEET DOUGHNUT DISKS

In a bowl, mix with wet hands:

> **2 cups white all-purpose flour**
> **½ cup ghee**
> **½ cup yogurt**
> **¼ teaspoon baking soda**

Knead well and let rest 10-30 minutes.

Form the dough into fourteen 1½" balls. Then flatten each ball between your palms into a 2" disk; make a central thumb-print depression in each disk. In a small frying pan, deep-fry the disks in ghee (or oil) until browned; remove and drain on paper towels.

Make a syrup by combining in a small saucepan over low heat:

> **¾ cup sugar**
> **½ cup water**

Let boil until it reaches 240° on a candy thermometer (three string stage). Dip the disks into the syrup, and turn several times so they can soak up some syrup. Remove to a serving dish. When all the disks are dipped, pour any left-over syrup over the top to make a glaze.

Makes 14
(traditional serving = 1)

Per serving: Calories: 163, Protein: 2 gm., Fat: 7 gm., Carbohydrates: 23 gm.

Fresh Ingredients
yogurt ½ cup

Other Ingredients
white all-purpose flour, 2 cups
ghee, ½ cup
baking soda, ¼ tsp
sugar, ¾ cup
ghee or vegetable oil for frying

Spices

BROWN SUGAR FUDGE

INDIAN FLAVORED FUDGE FROM INDIAN BROWN SUGAR, CHAPATI FLOUR, AND GHEE

Makes 2 dozen
(traditional serving = 1)

*Per serving: Calories: 75,
Protein: 1 gm., Fat: 4 gm.,
Carbohydrates: 9 gm.*

Fresh Ingredients

Other Ingredients
*Indian whole wheat flour,
1 cup
ghee, ½ cup
brown sugar, preferably
Indian, 1 cup*

Spices

Mix in a saucepan over low heat, stirring constantly:
> **1 cup Indian whole wheat flour (also called
> "chapati flour"), or whole wheat pastry flour
> ½ cup ghee**

Cook for about 5 minutes, until slightly browned.

Add:
> **1 cup brown sugar, preferably Indian brown sugar**

Cook, stirring constantly, until all the sugar is just melted,
about 5 minutes.

Press into an 8" round cake pan or pie plate greased with
ghee, using the back of a bowl or cup to knead until shiny.
Cut into 1" diamonds immediately. Let cool, then remove
from the pan in pieces.

CARROT BURFI

Sweet Halva Squares Made From Shredded Carrot Cooked in Milk

Place in a heavy-bottomed saucepan or the top of a double boiler:

2 cups carrots, shredded
1½ cups whole milk
1 cup heavy cream
½ cup sugar
2 Tablespoons butter

Bring to a boil and simmer uncovered on low heat for 2 hours, stirring occasionally. If you're using a double boiler, check the water level in the bottom from time to time.

After the first 2 hours of simmering, add:

½ cup dried milk powder
¼ cup ground, unsalted mixed nuts (almond, cashew, pistachio) (opt.)
pinch saffron-colored powder or turmeric (opt., for color)

Continue to simmer on low heat for another 1-3 hours until the volume is reduced to about one-third and the mixture is very thick. Be patient with this dessert. It does not require much attention for the first 1½ hours, but will need to be watched and stirred more frequently as the mixture thickens to prevent scorching. Grease an 8" round cake pan or pie plate with ghee, and spread the carrot mixture in it. Let cool, then cut into 1½" squares. You can also decorate it with whole almonds and cashews.

This can be eaten warm or cold; it will become more firm the cooler it gets. If you eat it warm, you will need a spoon to manage it.

Makes about 2½ cups
(traditional serving = ¼ cup)

Per serving: Calories: 181, Protein: 4 gm., Fat: 10.7 gm., Carbohydrates: 16 gm.

Fresh Ingredients
carrots, 2 cups shredded
whole milk, 1½ cups
heavy cream, 1 cup
butter, 2 TBS

Other Ingredients
sugar, ½ cup
dried milk powder, ½ cup
unsalted nuts, ¼ cup mixed

Spices
(optional: saffron-colored
powder or turmeric, pinch)

CHICKPEA SWEET BALLS

Sweet, Spiced Balls of Chickpea Flour

Makes 6 dozen
(traditional serving = 1-2)

*Per serving: Calories: 79,
Protein: 1 gm., Fat: 3.9 gm.,
Carbohydrates: 10 gm.*

Fresh Ingredients

Other Ingredients
chickpea flour, 1½ cups
*vegetable oil, ½ cup
ghee, ⅓ - ½ cup
(optional: almond, powdered,
    to taste)
granulated sugar, 2 cups*

Spices
cardamom powder, ½ tsp

Mix together in a large saucepan:
> **2½ cups chickpea flour***
> **½ cup vegetable oil**
> **⅓-½ cup ghee**
> **powdered almond (opt.)**

Sauté over low heat, stirring frequently, for 20-25 minutes until softened to the consistency of peanut butter and slightly browned.

Take off the heat and cool for about 5 minutes, then add:
> **2 cups granulated sugar**
> **½ teaspoon cardamom powder**

Mix well. Let cool for as long as possible, at least 30-60 minutes. The balls are easier to form when the ingredients are room temperature. Make into 1" balls by squeezing about 1 heaping teaspoon of dough back and forth from one hand to another. Continue this process until each ball is firm and shiny. The mixture will be crumbly at first, and it takes a number of passes between your hands for the ball to form. If you are finding the mixture too crumbly, be sure you have let it cool enough. Some people find using a melon baller helps the process. As a last resort, add a *little* more melted ghee.

*or equal parts uncooked cream of wheat and all-purpose white flour

CHIKKI
SESAME BRITTLE

Prepare a large counter-top or table for rolling-out the hot brittle by cleaning it well and oiling it lightly.

Combine in a saucepan:
> **1 cup brown sugar, Indian if possible***
> **1 teaspoon ghee**

Heat, *stirring constantly*, until the sugar is melted, then add:
> **¼ teaspoon baking soda**

Continue to heat (stirring constantly or the mixture will burn) until a tiny amount of mixture dripped onto the surface of the stove is crunchy as it cools—265° on a candy thermometer or the "hard-ball stage." The mixture will be dark brown.

Now quickly stir in:
> **2 cups roasted sesame seeds**
> **¼ cup roasted peanuts, chopped**

Pour out onto the prepared surface, and roll out *quickly* and vigorously into a thin layer with an oiled rolling pin. The mixture will become brittle as it cools. Break into pieces and put on a serving dish.

If you have difficulty with cleanup, you can pour boiling water over your pan or spoon to melt the hardened sugar.

* White sugar also works well, but the flavor will be more bland.

Makes about 1 lb.
(traditional serving = 1 oz.)

Per serving: Calories: 157, Protein: 4 gm., Fat: 9.2 gm., Carbohydrates: 13 gm.

Fresh Ingredients

Other Ingredients
brown sugar, Indian if possible, 1 cup*
ghee, 1 tsp
baking soda, ¼ tsp
sesame seeds, roasted, 2 cups
peanuts, roasted, unsalted, ¼ cup

Spices

COCONUT BURFI
Sweet Squares Made From Fresh Coconut Cooked in Milk

Makes 12
(traditional serving = 1)

Per serving: Calories: 346,
Protein: 3 gm., Fat: 23 gm.,
Carbohydrates: 31 gm.

Fresh Ingredients
whole milk,* ½ cup
coconut, fresh if possible,
  2 cups

Other Ingredients
sugar, 1½ cups

Spices
cardamom powder, 1½ tsp
(optional: saffron-colored
  powder, pinch)

Butter an 8" round cake or pie pan; set aside.

Cook together over medium heat:
  1½ cups sugar
  ½ cup whole milk*

Simmer, stirring constantly, until the mixture makes a single thread when pinched between 2 fingers—about 226° on a candy thermometer.

Then add:
  2 cups shredded, unsweetened coconut (preferably
    fresh)*
  1½ teaspoons cardamom powder
  pinch saffron-colored powder (opt. just for color)

Simmer over low heat, stirring constantly, for 5 minutes. Press the mixture into the buttered pan not quite to the edges and about ¾" thick; let cool. Cut into 1½" diamonds.

*A lower-fat milk can also be used, but the resulting mixture will be more crumbly. Fresh coconut is much better than dried in this recipe, but either form is acceptable.

CREAM OF WHEAT BALLS

SWEET BALLS MADE WITH CREAM OF WHEAT, SPICES, AND NUTS

Mix together in a saucepan:
> **1 cup uncooked cream of wheat**
> **1 cup all-purpose flour**
> **½ cup ghee**

Cook over a low flame until the mixture turns brown (about 5-10 minutes), then mix in and stir constantly for another 2-3 minutes:
> **1 cup sugar**
> **2 teaspoons powdered, unsalted nuts**
> **(mixture of cashew, pistachio, almond)**
> **1 teaspoon cardamom powder**

Mix well. Let cool for as long as possible, at least 30-60 minutes. The balls are easier to form when the ingredients are room temperature. Make into 1" balls by squeezing about 1 heaping teaspoon of dough back and forth from one hand to another. Continue this process until each ball is firm and shiny. The mixture will be crumbly at first, and it takes a number of passes between your hands for the ball to form. If you are finding the mixture too crumbly, be sure you have let it cool enough. Some people find using a melon baller helps the process. As a last resort, add a *little* more melted ghee.

Makes about 5 dozen
(traditional serving = 1-2)

Per serving: Calories: 60, Protein: 1 gm., Fat: 2.4 gm., Carbohydrates: 9 gm.

Fresh Ingredients

Other Ingredients
cream of wheat, uncooked 1 cup
all-purpose flour, 1 cup
ghee, ½ cup
sugar, 1 cup
mixed nuts, unsalted, 2 tsp, (cashew, pistachio, almond)

Spices
cardamom powder, 1 tsp

CREAM OF WHEAT HALVA

THICK CREAM OF WHEAT PUDDING WITH MILK AND NUTS

Makes 2 cups
(traditional serving = 3 TBS)

Per serving: Calories: 158, Protein: 2 gm., Fat: 4.6 gm., Carbohydrates: 27 gm.

Fresh Ingredients
butter, 2 TBS
whole milk, 1-1¼ cups

Other Ingredients
cream of wheat, uncooked
*   1 cup*
sugar, 1 cup
almonds, raw or roasted,
*   1 TBS*
cashews, raw or roasted,
*   1 TBS*
ghee, 2 tsp
(optional: yellow raisins, to
*   taste)*

Spices
cardamom powder, 1 tsp

In a saucepan over low heat, cook together until lightly browned and dry (about 5-10 minutes):

> **1 cup uncooked cream of wheat**
> **2 Tablespoons butter**

Stir in, a small amount at a time:

> **1-1¼ cups room temperature milk or water**

Stir in:

> **1 cup sugar**
> **1 Tablespoon raw or roasted almonds, in large pieces**
> **1 Tablespoon raw or roasted cashews, in large pieces**
> **1 teaspoon cardamom powder**
> **2 teaspoons ghee**
> **yellow raisins to taste (opt.)**

Cook, stirring continuously, for about 2 minutes or until sticky.

Eat with a spoon.

FLUFFY HALVA
Fluffy Cream of Wheat Pudding

In a medium-sized saucepan, heat:
>**1 Tablespoon + 1 teaspoon ghee**
>**⅔ cup uncooked cream of wheat**

Stirring frequently over low heat, cook until the cream of wheat has lightly browned, about 5-10 minutes. Remove from the pan and set aside.

In another saucepan, heat together to a brisk boil:
>**2 cups water**
>**½-⅔ cup sugar**
>**¾ teaspoon cardamom powder**

Mix in the browned cream of wheat. Cover, turn the heat to very low, and cook for 5-10 minutes. Check now and then to see if the mixture is thickening, but do not disturb the mixture much.

When thickened, remove from the heat. The mixture will thicken more as it cools.

If you wish, you can mix in any or all of the ingredients below just before serving:
>**2 teaspoons raisins**
>**2 teaspoons almonds, coarsely chopped**
>**2 teaspoons cashews, coarsely chopped**

Makes 2-3 cups
(traditional serving = 3 TBS)

Per serving: Calories: 109, Protein: 1 gm., Fat: 1.2 gm., Carbohydrates: 24 gm.

• • • •

Fresh Ingredients

Other Ingredients
ghee, 1 TBS + 1 tsp
cream of wheat, uncooked,
*   ⅔ cup*
sugar, ½-⅔ cup
(optional: raisins, 2 tsp)
(optional: almonds, 2 tsp)
(optional: cashews, 2 tsp)

Spices
cardamom powder, ¾ tsp

GULABJAMUN
MILKBALLS IN SWEET SYRUP

Makes about 18
(traditional serving = 2 balls with syrup)

Per serving: Calories: 509, Protein: 10 gm., Fat: 16.4 gm., Carbohydrates: 78 gm.

• • • •

Fresh Ingredients
heavy cream, 1½ cups

Other Ingredients
sugar, 3 cups
powdered milk, 2 cups
all-purpose flour, ⅔ cup
baking soda, 1 tsp
vegetable oil for deep frying

Spices
cardamom powder, 2 tsp
saffron, ¼ teaspoon

Make a syrup by boiling together until the sugar dissolves:
> **3 cups sugar**
> **7 cups water**

Turn off the heat and add:
> **2 teaspoons cardamom powder**
> **¼ teaspoon saffron**

Set the syrup aside in the saucepan on the stove.

Mix by hand in a bowl:
> **2 cups powdered milk**
> **⅔ cup all-purpose flour**
> **1 teaspoon baking soda**

Gradually mix in to form a soft dough (only slightly sticky):
> **1½ cups (or less) heavy cream**

Make into walnut-sized balls (you may use a small amount of cream on your hands while rolling); set aside and cover with a damp cloth.

Heat in a deep frying pan or wok:
> **4 cups vegetable oil**

Add the milkballs a few at a time in a basket. Fry to an even dark brown, shaking the basket continuously. (Adjust the heat so they don't get dark any sooner than 5-7 minutes.) When browned, drain the oil off of the milkballs, dip them into the syrup, then transfer onto a serving dish. (Re-boil the syrup between batches to keep the thickening process happening.)

After all the balls have been prepared, boil the syrup again for about 15 minutes, until thicker, and pour over the milkballs. Let the syrup soak in for a few hours before serving.

Serve hot or cold. This may be re-heated from the refrigerator (or freezer) by pouring hot syrup over the (defrosted) milkballs. They may also be topped with whipped cream.

INDIAN FRUIT SALAD
FRUIT SALAD WITH SURPRISING SPICES

In a bowl, combine the following fruits, chopped into bite-sized pieces:

> **1 pear**
> **1 apple**
> **1 mango**
> **1 papaya**
> **1 cup pineapple, fresh or canned**
> **1 cup strawberries**
> **1 cup grapes, halved**
> **1 large banana**

This should yield about 6 cups of chopped fruit. If you have more or less, adjust the amount of spices below accordingly. You can substitute other fruits as your taste and seasonal availability dictate.

Add:

> **2 Tablespoons sugar**
> **2 teaspoons chat masala***
> **2 teaspoons roasted cumin seeds, finely ground**
> **2 teaspoons lime juice**
> **½-1 teaspoon hot red pepper powder**
> **½ teaspoon salt**

*Chat masala is a distinctive mixture of spices sold ready-mixed in most Indian stores. It keeps quite well in an air-tight container. Chat masala can be an acquired taste; you may omit it.

Makes 6 cups
(traditional serving = ½ cup)

Per serving: Calories: 73, Protein: 1 gm., Fat: 0 gm., Carbohydrates: 17 gm.

• • • •

Fresh Ingredients
pear, 1
apple, 1
mango, 1
papaya, 1
pineapple, 1 cup fresh or
*   canned*
strawberries, 1 cup
grapes, 1 cup
banana, 1 large
lime juice, 2 tsp

Other Ingredients
sugar, 2 TBS
salt, ½ tsp

Spices
chat masala,* 2 tsp
cumin seeds, roasted, 2 tsp
hot red pepper powder,
*   ½-1 tsp*

LADDU
WHOLE WHEAT FLOUR SWEET BALLS

Mix together *very* well in a flat, shallow bowl or pan:
> **2 cups Indian whole wheat flour,**
> > **or whole wheat pastry flour**
>
> **½ cup uncooked cream of wheat**
> **2 Tablespoons ghee**

Add hot tap water (about ¼-½ cup) a little at a time to make a stiff, dry dough. Knead until it holds together. Divide the dough into 24 one-inch balls. Use your palms to press the dough into patties that are about 2 inches in diameter and ¼ inch thick.

Deep fry the patties in oil until browned. Drain and crumble them up while they are still hot. Put the pieces into a blender or food processor, and grind to the consistency of bread crumbs.

Mix the crumbs by hand with:
> **⅔ cup ghee (mix in half at a time)**
> **½-¾ cup sugar**
> **1 Tablespoon cardamom powder**

Squeeze about 1 heaping teaspoon of the crumb mixture back and forth from one hand to another. Continue this process until each ball is firm and shiny. The mixture will be crumbly at first, and it takes a number of passes between your hands for the ball to form. If you are finding the mixture too crumbly, let it cool longer. Some people find using a melon baller helps the process. As a last resort, add a *little* more melted ghee.

Makes 3 dozen
(traditional serving = 1-2)

Per serving: Calories: 115, Protein: 1 gm., Fat: 6.3 gm., Carbohydrates: 13 gm.

• • • •

Fresh Ingredients

Other Ingredients
Indian whole wheat flour, 2 cups
cream of wheat, uncooked, ½ cup
ghee, 2 TBS and ⅔ cup
vegetable oil, 1½ cups for deep-frying
sugar, ½ -¾ cup

Spices
cardamom powder, 1 TBS

FLUFFY MYSORE PAK
FLUFFY, RICH PEANUT SQUARES

Makes about 20
(traditional serving = 2)

*Per serving: Calories: 336,
Protein: 3 gm., Fat: 22 gm.,
Carbohydrates: 29 gm.*

• • • •

Fresh Ingredients

Other Ingredients
*roasted peanuts, 1 cup
ghee, 1½ cups
sugar, 1½ cups*

Spices

In a blender or food processor, coarsely grind (or place nuts in a plastic bag and crush with a rolling pin):
1 cup roasted peanuts

In a small saucepan on low heat, warm:
1½ cups ghee

In a separate larger saucepan, heat:
1½ cups sugar
¾ cup water

Bring this sugar-water to a boil, and cook until at the "single thread" stage—226° on a candy thermometer.

Now add:
the ground peanuts

Continue to cook, stirring constantly, until the mixture starts to pull away from the sides of the pan. Now add the warmed ghee, about 2 Tablespoons at a time, stirring constantly. The mixture will be fluffy. Turn the contents of the saucepan into a fine strainer for a few minutes to drain out the extra ghee. When there is only a slow drip of ghee from the strainer, turn the mixture out onto paper towels (to absorb the remaining ghee), and while still warm, shape into a 7½" round patty ¾" thick; slice into 1" diamonds. Let cool.

This dessert can be kept in the freezer or in an airtight plastic container in pantry.

MYSORE PAK
CHICKPEA FLOUR SWEET SQUARES

In a large bowl, place:
2 cups chickpea flour

In a saucepan, melt and continue to heat until steaming:
2 cups ghee

In another saucepan, heat together into a syrup:
1½ cups sugar
½ cup water

When the syrup is at the thread stage (226° on a candy thermometer), add 1 cup of the ghee to the flour, (keeping the rest of the ghee on low heat), and stir the flour mixture until there are no lumps. Add the flour and ghee mixture to the syrup, and stir *constantly* until the mixture pulls away from the sides of the pan when stirred and is very thick and lightly browned—about 5 minutes.

Remove from the heat. Add another cup of the ghee, a little at a time, then let mixture rest. Sprinkle with a tablespoon of warm milk.

Pour into a colander to drain off the excess ghee, then transfer to a baking pan. Flatten with the back of a measuring cup; cut into 1" diamonds, then flip out (upside-down) onto paper towels to absorb any remaining ghee.

Makes 32
(traditional serving = 1-2)

Per serving: Calories: 224, Protein: 1 gm., Fat: 15.7 gm., Carbohydrates: 18 gm.

• • • •

Fresh Ingredients
milk, 1 TBS

Other Ingredients
chickpea flour, 2 cups
ghee, 2 cups
sugar, 1½ cups

Spices

NOODLE PAYASAM
Delicately Seasoned Pudding with Rice Noodle Vermicelli

Makes 2 cups
(traditional serving = 3 TBS)

*Per serving: Calories: 79,
Protein: 3 gm., Fat: 2.9 gm.,
Carbohydrates: 9 gm.*

• • • •

Fresh Ingredients
whole milk, 1 quart

Other Ingredients
*rice vermicelli, super-fine,
    2 TBS
sugar, ¼ cup
(optional: cashews, unsalted)
(optional: raisins)
(optional: butter to sauté
    nuts and raisins)*

Spices
*cardamom powder, ½ tsp
saffron, pinch*

In a large, heavy-bottomed saucepan or the top of a double boiler, sauté in ghee for a few seconds:
> **2 Tablespoons super-fine rice vermicelli**

Add:
> **1 quart whole milk**
> **¼ cup sugar**
> **½ teaspoon cardamom powder**
> **pinch saffron**
> **unsalted cashew nuts and/or raisins, fried in a
>   little butter (opt.)**

Continue simmering over low heat, stirring periodically, until thickened and reduced to about half the volume — about 1-2 hours. If using a double boiler, check the water level in the bottom of the pan now and then.

Be patient with this dessert—the thickening takes time. Low-fat milk does not thicken as well as whole milk does.

PEDHA
Powdered Milk Fudge

In a large, heavy saucepan, mix together over low heat:
> **¼ cup unsalted butter**
> **½ cup milk**
> **½ cup heavy cream**
> **½ cup sugar**
> **1 teaspoon cardamom powder**

Let boil, stirring frequently, until thickened (about 5-10 minutes).

Add:
> **2 cups powdered milk (enough powder for 2 quarts of milk)**

Mix very thoroughly over low heat for 2 minutes, then remove from the heat. The mixture will be very stiff and dry. Let cool until it can be handled easily. Roll into 1" balls, then flatten gently to 1½" rounds.

Dust lightly with:
> **confectioners' sugar.**

Makes 2½ dozen
(traditional serving = 2)

Per serving: Calories: 178, Protein: 5 gm., Fat: 10.3 gm., Carbohydrates: 15 gm.

• • • •

Fresh Ingredients
butter, unsalted, ¼ cup
milk, ½ cup
heavy cream, ½ cup

Other Ingredients
sugar, ½ cup
powdered milk, 2 cups
confectioners' sugar, to sprinkle

Spices
cardamom powder, 1 tsp

RASMALAI
Sweet Ricotta Squares with Nuts and Creamy Sauce

Makes 2 dozen
(traditional serving = 2)

*Per serving: Calories: 245,
Protein: 8 gm., Fat: 15.2 gm.,
Carbohydrates: 17 gm.*

• • • •

Fresh Ingredients
*ricotta cheese, 16 ounces
(2 cups)
half-and-half, 2 cups*

Other Ingredients
*sugar, ½-1 cup
almonds (or other nuts),
1 cup
vanilla extract, 1 tsp*

Spices
*(optional: cardamom powder,
¼ tsp)
(optional: saffron, ¼ tsp)*

In a bowl, mix together until very smooth:
>**16 ounces (2 cups) ricotta cheese**
>**½-1 cup sugar**

Pour into an 8" square baking dish, and place in a preheated 350° oven for 20 minutes. Continue to bake another 10-20 minutes, checking the mixture every 5 minutes until it separates from the sides of the pan. Remove and cool.

Bring to a boil in a saucepan:
>**2 cups half and half**
>**¼ teaspoon cardamom powder (opt.)**
>**¼ teaspoon saffron (opt.)**

Cut the baked ricotta into serving-sized squares, and place in a deep serving dish.

Sprinkle with:
>**1 teaspoon vanilla extract**

Pour the half and half evenly over the squares, and allow to soak.

Serve topped with:
>**1 cup slivered unsalted almonds (or unsalted
>   pistachios, unsalted walnuts, or a mixture
>   of those nuts)**

If you want to decrease the richness of this dessert, you can use regular or 2% milk instead of half and half in the sauce. Your sauce will be thinner, but will still be tasty. You can also substitute non-fat ricotta; the texture will be drier, but the dessert will still be flavorful.

RICE PAYASAM
DELICATELY SEASONED RICE PUDDING

Boil together over a low flame in a heavy saucepan or in the top of a double boiler:

> **1 quart whole milk**
> **1½ Tablespoons uncooked rice**

Stir periodically.

After the rice has simmered for about 20 minutes and is soft, add:

> **¼ cup sugar**
> **½ teaspoon cardamom powder**
> **pinch saffron**
> **unsalted cashew nuts and/or raisins, fried in a**
> **little butter (opt.)**

Continue simmering over low heat, stirring periodically, until thickened and reduced to about half the volume—about 1 to 2 hours. If using a double boiler, check the water level now and then.

Be patient with this dessert—the thickening takes time. Low-fat milk does not thicken as well as whole milk does.

Makes 2 cups
(traditional serving = 3 TBS)

Per serving: Calories: 77, Protein: 3 gm., Fat: 2.9 gm., Carbohydrates: 9 gm.

• • • •

Fresh Ingredients
whole milk, 1 quart

Other Ingredients
rice, uncooked, 1½ TBS
sugar, ¼ cup
(optional: unsalted cashews)
(optional: raisins)
(optional: butter for sautéing nuts and raisins)

Spices
cardamom powder, ½ tsp
saffron, pinch

ROASTED CHICKPEA SQUARES

SWEET, SPICED SQUARES MADE FROM ROASTED CHICKPEAS

Makes 15
(traditional serving = 2)

Per serving: Calories: 126, Protein: 2 gm., Fat: 3.1 gm., Carbohydrates: 22 gm.

• • • •

Fresh Ingredients

Other Ingredients
sugar, ⅔ cup
roasted chickpeas, 1 cup
ghee, 1 TBS
white Indian poppy seeds,*
* 1 TBS*
unsweetened coconut, 1 TBS

Spices
cardamom powder, 1 tsp

In a blender, grind to a powder:
1 cup roasted dry chickpeas

In a small saucepan, make a sugar syrup by combining:
⅔ cup sugar
½ cup water

Simmer until you reach the "thread stage" (226° on a candy thermometer).

Working quickly, immediately take off the heat, add, and mix well:
the powdered roasted chickpeas
1 teaspoon cardamom powder

Add quickly and mix well:
1 Tablespoon ghee

Quickly and firmly press the mixture into a 7" circle about ¼" thick on a greased, flat pan. Sprinkle with:
1 Tablespoon white Indian poppy seeds*
1 Tablespoon unsweetened coconut

Let cool; cut into 1½" diamonds and serve. Sometimes this comes out crumbly, but it will still taste delicious.

* Can be omitted—do not substitute black poppy seeds

SHANKAR PALLA
Sweet Fried Dough

In a shallow pan or bowl, mix by hand until very smooth (about 5 minutes):

> ¼ cup water
> ¼ cup sugar
> ¼ cup vegetable oil

Add:

> **2 cups all-purpose flour**

Use enough flour to make a very stiff dough, similar to rolled cookie dough. Roll out one-half of the dough at a time into a 12" circle. Cut into 1" diamonds.

Deep-fry the pieces of dough in small batches (6-8) in a deep fryer or wok until browned.

Serve with *Dosa Chutney*, pg. 39.

Makes 8 dozen
(traditional serving = 6)

Per serving: Calories: 91, Protein: 2 gm., Fat: 3.3 gm., Carbohydrates: 14 gm.

• • • •

Fresh Ingredients

Other Ingredients
sugar, ¼ cup
vegetable oil, ¼ cup and for deep frying
all-purpose flour, 2 cups

Spices

SHEERA

Sweetened Whole Wheat Flour Porridge, Sprinkled with Coconut

Makes 3 cups
(traditional serving = 3 TBS)

*Per serving: Calories: 127,
Protein: 1 gm., Fat: 8.5 gm.,
Carbohydrates: 11 gm.*

• • • •

Fresh Ingredients
*unsalted butter, ½ cup +
2 TBS*

Other Ingredients
*Indian whole wheat flour,
1 cup
sugar, ½ cup
coconut, unsweetened, to top*

Spices
cardamom powder, 1 tsp

In a saucepan over medium heat, mix into a paste:
> **1 cup Indian whole wheat flour, or whole wheat
> pastry flour**
> **½ cup + 2 Tablespoons unsalted butter**

Sauté until slightly browned.

Add and stir well:
> **1 cup water**
> **½ cup sugar**
> **1 teaspoon cardamom powder**

Cover the pan and turn off the heat.

Serve sprinkled with:
> **unsweetened, shredded coconut**

Eat with a spoon.

SRIKHAND

SWEET, THICKENED YOGURT WITH DELICATE SEASONING AND POWDERED NUTS

Place in a cheesecloth:
> **3½ cups (2 lbs.) whole milk plain yogurt***

Let hang from the kitchen faucet for about 3 hours or until all the liquid has drained. Pull the yogurt through the cheese-cloth into a bowl. Alternately, you can line a fine sieve with cheesecloth or a clean white cotton handkerchief, and let the yogurt drain that way.

Add:
> **¼ cup mixed unsalted almonds/cashews/**
> **pistachios, powdered**
> **5 whole cardamoms, peeled and powdered,**
> **or 1 tsp. ground cardamom**
> **¼ tsp. powdered saffron**
> **½ cup sugar (more or less, to taste)**

Mix well and chill.

Some people prefer this dessert with less cardamom. It can be eaten with fresh or canned fruits, topped over gelatin and pies, or by itself.

*You can make this dessert with low-fat or even non-fat yogurt, and it will still taste very good.

Makes about 2 cups
(traditional serving =
3-4 TBS)

Per serving: Calories: 121,
Protein: 4 gm., Fat: 4.7 gm.,
Carbohydrates: 15 gm.

• • • •

Fresh Ingredients
*yogurt, whole milk, plain,**
3½ cups (2 lbs.)

Other Ingredients
almond/cashew/pistachio
nuts unsalted, ¼ cup
sugar, ½ cup

Spices
cardamoms, 5 whole or 1 tsp
powder
saffron, ¼ tsp

SWEET CHIROTE

RICH WHITE FLOUR ROUNDS, FRIED AND DUSTED WITH CONFECTIONERS' SUGAR

Makes 16
(traditional serving = 1)

Per serving: Calories: 70,
Protein: 2 gm., Fat: 2.3 gm.,
Carbohydrates: 11 gm.

• • • •

Fresh Ingredients

Other Ingredients
all-purpose flour, 2 cups
ghee, 2 TBS and for kneading
rice flour, pinch
vegetable oil, for frying
confectioners' sugar, for
* sprinkling*

Spices

In a flat pan (easier than a bowl), mix together with your fingers:

> **2 cups white all-purpose flour**
> **1 Tablespoon ghee**

Gradually add warm water (about ½ cup), mixing well to form a dough.

Knead well. Add about 1 teaspoon more ghee, and knead until very smooth. Pinch off lemon-sized balls and flatten, then roll out to 5" circles.

Mix together in a small bowl with fingers:

> **1 Tablespoon ghee**
> **pinch rice flour**

Spread some of this mixture onto one circle, and top with another circle. Spread with more ghee mixture. Continue to add circles and top with ghee until all the circles are used. Roll up tightly like a jelly roll. Roll the tube on a flat surface until it is 12 inches long and 1 inch wide. Slice into ¾ inch slices. Roll these into 3 inch circles.

Deep-fry in vegetable oil, pressing with a spatula so the inner layers will cook well. Flip over when the top side is white and puffy when pressed with spatula.

Shake the finished chirote in a paper bag until well coated with:

> **confectioners's sugar**

SWEET SHANKIR PALLA

Sweet, Puffy Fried Dough in a Sugar Syrup

In a bowl, mix:

1 cup all-purpose white flour
2½ Tablespoons vegetable oil
⅛-¼ cup water, enough to make a soft dough

Cover the dough and let rest a few minutes. Roll out the dough in a large, thin circle on a bare surface. Cut the dough into diamonds, and peel off of the rolling surface with a spatula.

Deep-fry the diamonds until browned, and drain.

In a very large saucepan, make a syrup out of:

1 cup sugar
½ cup water

Cook over high heat until boiling, then simmer until at the two-thread stage (about 230° on a candy thermometer). Add the fried dough squares to the syrup in the saucepan, and toss until uniformly covered with syrup. (The syrup will begin to look like white crystals as you mix them.)

Let cool slightly, and serve.

Makes 4 dozen
(traditional serving = 3)

*Per serving: Calories: 89,
Protein: 1 gm., Fat: 2 gm.,
Carbohydrates: 16 gm.*

• • • •

Fresh Ingredients

Other Ingredients
*all-purpose flour, 1 cup
vegetable oil, 2½ TBS and
    for deep frying
sugar, 1 cup*

Spices

PANTRY SET-UP AND GLOSSARY OF UNUSUAL INGREDIENTS

If you have these ingredients on hand, you will only need to buy the fresh ingredients to make almost any recipe in this book.

SPICES

Ajama seeds—also called oregano seeds

Amchur powder—made from mangoes, optional, because it can be replaced by lemon juice (in twice the amount)

Bay leaves, Indian if possible—Indian ones can be eaten, but regular ones must be removed

Cardamom, whole and ground

Cinnamon, whole and ground

Cloves, whole and ground

Coriander, ground

Cumin, seeds and ground—some recipes call for roasted cumin seeds; you can do this easily in a dry pan

Cumin/coriander powder—a one-to-one mixture; you can buy this ready-made or make your own stock

Fenugreek seeds—used mostly in chutneys in this book

Garam masala—a combination of powdered spices which can be bought ready-made in Indian and other stores

Ginger, ground

Hing (optional)—also called asafoetida, a sulfurous spice used in tiny amounts. It can be omitted.

Hot peppers—whole dried, and ground hot red pepper powder (any variety will do, but each is differently hot)

Mustard seeds—black, not yellow

Pav Bahji masala—another combination of powdered spices which can be bought ready-made

Peppercorns, whole

Saffron threads—expensive but used in tiny amounts

Saffron-colored powder—sometimes called saffron powder; optional since it is used only to give yellow color

Salt

Seeds mixture—make your own stock with 1 part cumin seeds, 2 parts mustard seeds, and 1 part sesame seeds

Sesame seeds

Tamarind paste—also called imli; a sweet fruit puree which keeps excellently for a long time in the refrigerator

Tea masala—a home-made mixture of spices used only in coffee and tea in this book (see pages 30-1)
Turmeric powder

STAPLES

Beans—your favorites, dried or canned; in most of these recipes, one kind can be substituted for another.
  black-eyed peas—can be used dried or canned
  chana (also, chickpeas, garbanzos)—can be used dried or canned
  lentils, oily—found in Indian stores, these must be rinsed before using
  yellow—can be substituted for oily, if desired, in any recipe
  brown or orange—used in lentil vegetable soup only, in this book
  mung beans, whole or split—usually can be substituted for lentils if desired
  urrad dal—a Indian legume used in a few recipes; hard to substitute but keeps forever
  yellow split peas—used in several of these recipes
Chickpea flour—also called besan, made from ground chickpeas
Coconut, unsweetened, shredded
Vegetable oil
Cream of wheat—any kind is fine, though Indian cream of wheat tastes a little different
Ghee, clarified unsalted, butter—see recipe on page 82. Keeps well unrefrigerated and even better cold.
Flour, white all-purpose
Indian whole wheat flour—also called chapati flour, or whole wheat pastry flour. An acceptable substitute is a mixture of equal parts whole wheat and white flour.
Nuts—cashew, almonds, and/or pistachios, all unsalted, are used in some desserts
Peanuts, roasted, unsalted—Indian ones are smaller and taste especially nice.
Roasted Indian chickpeas—used in several dishes and snacks
Rice flour
Sugar, white and brown—If you can get Indian brown sugar, it has a unique taste.

SAMPLE MENUS

Menu 1
Yogurt Soup, pg. 23
Potato Curry, pg. 141
plain rice
Puris, pg. 71
Tamarind-Date Chutney, pg. 46
Cucumber Raita, pg. 56
Lime Pickle, pg. 57
Srikhand, pg. 175

Menu 2
Pakora, pg. 95
Chana, pg. 104
Rice Pilaf, pg. 87
Puris or Self-rising Puris, pgs. 71-2
Apple Butter Chutney, pg. 36
Cucumber Raita, pg. 56
Indian Fruit Salad, pg. 164

Menu 3
Tomato Vegetable, pg. 146
Spicy Mung Beans, pg. 111
plain rice
Chapati, pg. 64
Green Tomato Chutney, pg. 41
Spinach Raita, pg. 59
Gulabjamon, pg. 162

Menu 4
Peanut Soup, pg. 22
Onion Vegetable, pg. 137
plain rice
Chapati, pg. 64
Cabbage Salad, pg. 54
Noodle Payasam, pg. 168

Menu 5
Brussels Sprouts, pg. 121
Black-eyed Pea Curry, pg. 102
plain rice
Puris, pg. 71
Peanut Chutney, pg. 45
Radish Pickle, pg. 58
Brown Sugar Fudge, pg. 154

Menu 6
Lentil Soup, pg. 17
Bharta, pg. 120
Rice Pilaf, pg. 87
Chapati, pg. 64
Mango Chutney, pg. 43
Rasmali, pg. 170

Menu 7
Mixed Vegetables, pg. 134
Lentils with Dill, pg. 107
Spinach (Saag) Paneer, pg. 144
plain rice
Chapati, pg. 64
Coconut Chutney, pg. 37
Rice Payasam, pg. 171

INDIAN GROCERY & SPECIALTY STORES

Below is a list of Indian grocery stores and other specialty food stores which carry some or all of the Indian spices and other ingredients mentioned in these recipes. Each of the stores in this list was asked for: verification of name, address and telephone; fax number; acceptance of credit cards; mail order policy (mo); and availability of a catalog. If a listing below does not show some of this information, it means that that item or service is not available at that store at this time (for example, acceptance of mail orders). We have taken every care to insure the accuracy of this information, but cannot guarantee it.

We have not visited every one of these stores, so we cannot give personal recommendations among them. All of them carry grocery items for Indian cooking. Feel free to call one or more stores for more information.

We include listings in most of the 50 United States, and across Canada, but we know that we have found only a fraction of existing Indian stores. If none of these listings are convenient for you, we suggest you look in your local Yellow Pages under "Grocers," "Specialty Food Stores," or "Health Food Stores." Some local Indian restaurants may be willing to suggest a local grocer.

Remember also that many of these stores are willing to send supplies to you by mail. You can select a store with less regard to its location when your purchase will be by mail. The following listings include information about acceptance of mail orders (mo) and whether there is a minimum order for the service. Different stores make different arrangements about payments and method of delivery which you can verify with them. If ordering by phone or mail, you can request that all your items be labeled in English.

ALABAMA
Chai's Store
2133 7th Avenue South
Birmingham, AL 35233
205-324-4873

ALASKA
Asian Mini-Mart
9328 Glacier Hwy, Suite 47B
Juneau, AK 99801
907-790-2742
mo ($30 min, orders shipped collect)

ARIZONA
Bombay Bazaar
334 E Camelback Road
Phoenix, AZ 85012-1614
602-265-8781
cash or check, mo ($50 min)

CALIFORNIA
Bazaar of India Imports
1810 University Avenue
Berkeley, CA 94703-1516
510-548-4110, 800-261-7662
Fax: 548-1115
Visa, MC, Amex, Disc, Diner
mo (no min, catalog $3.00 [refndbl])

India Spice House
6715-H Dublin Blvd
Dublin, CA 94568
510-551-5332
Credit cards to be accepted in future, mo ($50 min.)

Guru Palace
5146 Mowry Ave.
Fremont, CA 94538
Tel: 510-791-7410, Fax: 791-1575
credit cards accepted
mo (COD, $25 min)

Tajmahal Imports
5113 Mowry Ave.
Fremont, CA 94538
Tel: 510-794-1000, Fax: 510-794-9789
Visa, MC, mo (no min)

Bezjian Grocery
4725 Santa Monica Blvd
Hollywood, CA 90029
Tel: (213) 663-1503

India Imports and Exports
3838 W 102 St
Inglewood, CA 90303
Tel: 310-330-8900, Fax: 310-677-6300
Check, COD, mo (no min)

Bombay Spiceland
8650 Reseda Blvd 4&5
Northridge, CA 91324
Tel: 818-701-9383, Fax: 818-701-5744
cash or check, mo ($50 min, flyer)

Spice Plus
PO Box 547
Novato, CA 94948
Tel: 415-499-1947, Fax: 415-883-7837
800-525-SPICE
MC Visa Disc Amex
"all" mo (no min, price list)

G.T. Sakai & Company
1313 Broadway
Sacramento, CA 95818
Tel: 916-446-7968, Fax: 446-2927

India Spice and Herb Bazaar
3060 Clairemont Dr.
San Diego, CA 92117
619-276-7226
mo (no min, price list on request)

Haig's Delicacies
642 Clement St
San Francisco, CA 94118
Tel & Fax: 415-752-6283
Visa, MC, mo ($20 min, catalog)

India Gifts and Food
907 Post St
San Francisco, CA 94109
Tel: 415-771-5041 Fax: 415-775-3304
mo (no min, catalog)

Bharat Bazaar
3680 El Camino Real
K-Mart Shopping Center
Lawrence & El Camino
Santa Clara, CA 95051
Tel: 408-247-4307, Fax: 510-656-0198
Visa, MC, mo ($40 min)

Guru Palace
1053 El Camino Rio, #9
Sunnyvale, CA 94087
408-554-8675

Tarver's Delicacies
De Anza Shopping Center
1338 South Mary Ave.
Sunnyvale, CA 94087
408-732-1892
mo (UPS, no min)

COLORADO
Tajmahal Imports
3095 C. South Peoria St.
Aurora, CO 80014
303-751-8571
Visa, MC, Disc, food stamps, check
or cash, mo (UPS, no min)

CONNECTICUT
India Spice and Gift Shop
3295 Fairfield Ave
Bridgeport, CT 06605
203-384-0666
Visa, MC, mo

Edge of the Woods Health Foods
379 Whalley Ave
New Haven, CT 06511
Tel: 203-787-1055, Fax: 203-787-6782
MC, Visa

Cosmos International
770 Farmington Ave
West Hartford, CT 06119-1615
203-232-6600
MC, Visa, Disc
mo ($25 min plus s&h)

International Foods
1565 South Main St
Waterbury, CT 06706
203-574-5356
Visa, MC
mo (UPS, no min)

DELAWARE
Indian Food and Appliances
222 W Market St
Newport, DE 19804
Tel & Fax: 302-998-1006
Visa, MC, Disc
mo ($25 min)

FLORIDA
Indian Grocery Store
2342 Douglas Rd
Coral Gables, FL 33134
305-448-5869
mo (no min, UPS COD w/ s&h)

Little Market
3062 N Andrews Ave
Ft Lauderdale, FL 33311
Tel & Fax: 305-561-8606

GEORGIA
Tajmahal Imports
1594 Woodcliff Dr #G
Atlanta, GA 30329
404-321-5940
mo (no min)

ILLINOIS
Apna Bazaar
2314 W Devon Ave
Chicago, IL 60659
Tel: 312-262-4200, Fax: 312-465-2755
MC, Visa
mo (UPS w/ UPS charges)

India Gifts and Foods
1031 W Belmont Ave
Chicago, IL 60657
Tel: 312-348-4392, Fax: 312-348-5241
MC, Visa, Amex
mo (UPS, no min, catalog)

India Gifts and Foods
53-55 North Maplewood Ave
Chicago, IL 60659
312-274-7979
MC, Visa, Amex
mo (UPS, no min, catalog)

International Food Market
7221 West Madison
Forest Park, IL 60130
Tel: 708-524-2626, Fax: 708-524-0083
MC, Visa, Disc, mo, no min, catalog

INDIANA
International Food Market
3839 Moller Rd
Indianapolis, IN 46254
317-291-5282
mo (no min)

IOWA
International Groceries
7517 Douglas Ave #16
Urbandale, IA 50322
515-278-1522
MC, Visa, Disc, mo (no min)

KANSAS
India Emporium
10458 Metcalf
Overland Park, KS 66212
Tel: 913-642-1161, Fax: 913-642-8312
MC, Visa, Disc, mo (no min)

India Emporium
3008 E Harry St.
Wichita, KS 67211
Tel: 316-687-3266, Fax: 316-683-5909
MC, Visa, Amex, Disc, mo (UPS)

LOUISIANA
India Imports
("International Market")
3601 Williams Blvd
Kenner, LA 70065
Tel: 504-443-3601, Fax: 504-443-1505
mo (no min)

MARYLAND
India Bazaar
9045 Gaither Rd.
Gaithersburg, MD 20877
301-840-9799

Sadana International
1355 Holton Lane
Langley Park, MD 20783
Tel: 301-434-2433, Fax: 301-434-2437
mo (no min, catalog)

MASSACHUSETTS
India Tea & Spice Inc.
453 Common Street
Belmont, MA 02178
Tel & Fax: 617-484-3737
mo ($25 min, catalog)

India Groceries
16 Tremont St., Oak Square
Brighton, MA 02135
617-254-5540
personal checks, mo (UPS, $25 min)

East West Foods
120 Cambridge St., Rt 3A
Burlington, MA 01803
617-229-2124

India Foods & Spices
80 River St.
Cambridge, MA 02139
Tel: 617-497-6144, Fax: 617-547-8644
MC, Visa, mo ($50 min, free local
delivery for $50 min order, catalog)

Concord Spice & Grain
93 Thoreau Street
Concord, MA 01742
Tel & Fax: 508-369-1535
MC, Visa, Disc, mo ($10 min)

MICHIGAN
Foods 'N Flavors
7260 Sheldon Road
Canton, MI 48187
313-455-0160
Visa, MC, mo

India Food and Boutique
30565 John R. Road
Madison Heights, MI 48071
810-585-7775
Visa, MC, mo (no min)

MINNESOTA
Patel Groceries and Video
1848 Central Avenue, N.E.
Minneapolis, MN 55418
612-789-8800
mo ($10 min plus postage)

MISSOURI
Seema Enterprises
52 Manchester Mall
Highway 141 & Manchester
Manchester, MO 63011
Tel: 314-391-5914, Fax: 314-423-0391
MC, Visa, Disc, mo (no min)

Seema Enterprises
10618 Page Avenue
St. Louis, MO 63132
Tel: 314-423-9990, Fax: 314-423-0391
MC, Visa, Disc, mo (no min)

MONTANA
Butterfly Herbs
232 North Higgins Avenue
Missoula, MT 59802
406-728-8780
Visa, MC, mo (no min, catalog)

NEBRASKA
Indian Groceries and Video
3029 South 83rd Plaza
Omaha, NE 68124
402-391-0844
mo (no min)

NEVADA
India Food and Spices
3661 Maryland Pkwy #69
Maryland Shopping Center
Las Vegas, NV 89109
Tel & Fax: 702-733-0640
mo ($30 min, price list)

NEW HAMPSHIRE
East West Foods
Lamplighter Square
Daniel Webster Highway
Nashua, NH 03062
Tel: 603-888-7521, Fax: 603-888-1232
mo (UPS, no min)

NEW JERSEY
Bharhat
557 River Road
Elmwood Park, NJ 07407
201-791-4070
mo ($20 min)

New India Groceries
76 West Palisade Avenue
Englewood, NJ 07631
201-568-9532
mo ($20 min)

International Foods, Inc.
1275 Bloomfield Avenue,
Bldg. #9, Door #76
Inside Pio Costa Complex
Fairfield, NJ 07004
Tel: 201-575-9575, 201-575-3534
Fax: 201-575-6820
MC, Visa, Disc
mo (UPS, no min)

Dana Bazaar
297 Central Avenue
Jersey City , NJ 07306
201-656-7396
mo ($50 min)

Taj Mahal
4811 Stelton Rd
S.Plainfield, NJ 07080
908-753-0620
mo (no min)

NEW MEXICO
India Kitchen
6910 Montgomery NE
Albuquerque, NM 87109
Tel: 505-884-2333, Fax: 505-292-9861
credit cards accepted
mo ($10 min)

NEW YORK
Brooklyn Indo-Pak Groceries
1034 Coney Island Ave
Brooklyn, NY 11230
718-434-0480

Patel Groceries
53-03 4th Avenue
Brooklyn, NY 11220
718-748-6369
mo (COD, money order, cert.check,)

Patel Groceries
3145 Coney Island Ave
Brooklyn, NY 11235
718-743-4318
mo (COD, money order, cert. check)

Dana Bazaar
42-69 Main St
Flushing, NY 11355
718-353-2818
mo (no min)

Dana Bazaar
73-12A 37th Ave.
Jackson Heights, NY 11372
Tel:718-779-1307,
Fax: 718-358-5123 (specify Dana
Bazaar)
mo (UPS, COD or pay in advance)

House of Spices
76-17 Broadway
Jackson Heights, NY 11373
tel: 718-476-1577, Fax: 718-507-4798
mo (no min, catalog)

Aphrodisia
264 Bleeker St
New York , NY 10014
212-989-6440
MC, Visa, Amex
mo (min: ¼ lb/item, call for price)

Foods of India
121 Lexington Ave.
New York, NY 10016
Tel: 212-683-4419, Fax: 212-251-0946
Visa, MC, Amex, Disc
mo (no min, catalog)

Kalustyan's
123 Lexington Ave
New York, NY 10016
212-685-3451, Fax: 212-683-8458
MC, Visa, Amex
mo (no min, catalog)

Original Little India Store
128 East 28th St
New York, NY 10016
Tel: 212-683-1691, Fax: 212-481-0383
MC, Visa, mo (no min)

Asian Groceries
2150 Central Park Ave
Yonkers, NY 10710
Tel & Fax: 914-793-6363
mo (no min, info on request)

Nick's Supermarket
454 South Broadway
Yonkers, NY 10705
914-963-6161
mo (no min)

NORTH CAROLINA
Wellspring Grocery
81 South Elliott Rd
Chapel Hill, NC 27514
Tel: 919-968-1983, Fax: 919-967-0228
Visa, MC

Payal Indian Grocery
6400 Pineville Rd.
Charlotte, NC 28217
704-521-9680

Talley's Green Grocery
1408 E Blvd.
Charlotte, NC 28203
Tel: 704-334-9200, Fax: 704-334-9204
Visa, MC, Disc

Taj Imports
2109-146 Avent Ferry Rd
Raleigh, NC 27606
Tel & Fax: 919-831-1111
mo (UPS or COD only, $20 min)

OHIO
India Groceries and Gifts
4412 Cleveland Ave.
Columbus, OH 43231
614-476-8555
Visa, MC, mo ($10 min)

India Food Emporium
1217 E 305
Willowick, OH 44092
Tel: 216-585-1835, Fax: 216-781-1701
mo

OREGON
India Emporium
SW Bvrtn Hillsdale Hwy
Beaverton, OR 97005
Tel: 503-646-0592, Fax: 503-690-6831
Visa, MC, mo (no min)

International Food Bazaar
915 SW 9th
Portland, OR 97205
Tel: 503-228-1960, Fax: 503-246-9596
credit cards, mo

PENNSYLVANIA
S&R Groceries
111 S 8th St
Allentown, PA 18102
215-821-8255
cash or check

Spice Smuggler
835 W Main St
Landsdale, PA 19446
215-362-8893
Visa, MC, Disc/$15 min.
mo ($15 min plus S&H, call for info)

India Foods & Exhibits
4141 Old Wm. Penn Highway
Monroeville, PA 15146
412-373-1571
mo (no min)

House of Spices
4605 N 6th St
Philadelphia, PA 19140
Tel: 215-455-6870, Fax: 215-455-3239
mo (COD, no min)

Spice Corner
904 S 9th St.
Philadelphia, PA 19147
Tel: 215-925-1660, Fax: 215-592-7430
Visa, MC, Disc
mo ($15 min, catalog)

Bombay Emporium
294 Craft Avenue
Pittsburg, PA 15213
Tel: 412-682-4965, Fax: 412-621-9008
mo ($15 min)

RHODE ISLAND
Not Just Spices
77 Burlington St
Providence, RI 02906
401-351-6555
mo (UPS, $20 min)

Spices 'n Things
1388 Mineral Spring Ave.
N.Providence, RI 02904
401-353-0105
mo (no min)

SOUTH CAROLINA
Touch of India
14 Diamond Lane
Columbia, SC 29210
803-731-5960
mo (no min)

TENNESSEE
Shubha Enterprises
2516 Nolensville Rd.
Nashville, TN 37211
615-242-0204
mo (no min)

TEXAS
Bombay Imports
13219 Bellaire Blvd
Houston, TX 77083
713-495-6674

India Grocers
9683 South West at Bissonnet
Houston, TX 77074
Tel: 713-270-1165, Fax: 713-484-4561
Visa, MC
mo (no min)

India Grocers
5604 Hillcroft
Houston, TX 77036
Tel: 713-782-8500, Fax: 713-484-4561
Visa, MC, Disc
mo (no min)

Tajmahal Imports
26-C Richardson Hghts Village
Richardson, TX 75080
Tel: 214-644-1329, Fax: 214-985-8094
Visa, MC, Disc, mo (no min)

UTAH
House of India Grocery & Spices
89-D St. 2nd Ave.
Salt Lake City, UT 84103
Tel: 801-531-1652, Fax: 801-975-0553
food stamps, mo (no min, UPS)

VIRGINIA
Bharat Gift and Spices
4231 C Markham St
Annandale, VA 22003
Tel & Fax: 703-256-9267
MC, Visa, Disc, mo ($40 min)

India Spice and Gifts
3901 Wilson Blvd
Arlington, VA 22203
Tel: 703-522-0149, Fax: 703-528-5603
Visa, MC, mo ($50 min)

Sadana International
3709 Columbia Pike
Arlington, VA 22204
Tel: 703-979-6262, Fax: 301-434-2437
credit cards accepted, mo (no min, catalog)

Bombay Store
7033 Brookfield Plaza
Springfield, VA 22150
Tel: 703-569-6777, Fax: 703-451-0332
MC, Visa, Amex

WASHINGTON
Singh's International Video & Spices
15920 NE 8th St. #4
Bellevue, WA 98008
206-643-0366
"name of store might change but address will be same"

Market Spice Retail Mail Order
PO Box 2935
Redmond, WA 98073-2935
206-883-1220
Visa, MC, Amex
mo only (no min, catalog)

Shanti Video and Groceries
757 Rainier Ave S, Ste 5
Renton, WA 98055
206-228-9659
mo ($100 min)

Ayengar Assoc.
2516 NE 95th St
Seattle, WA 98155-2428
Tel: 206-524-4040, Fax: 206-527-5993
MC, Visa, mo (catalog and/or product price list , free shipping with $100 min, 50 lb max, & pay in advance)

Market Spice
85A Pike Place
Seattle, WA 98101
206-622-6340
Visa, MC, Amex
mo (no min, catalog)

The Souk
1916 Pike Place Market
Seattle, WA 98101
Tel: 206-441-1666, Fax: 206-367-8387
Visa, MC, mo ($30 min, catalog)

The Souk
11730 Pinehurst Way NE
Seattle, WA 98125
206-367-8387
Visa, MC, mo ($30 min, catalog)

WEST VIRGINIA
Taste of India
1011 Quarrier St
Charleston, WV 25301
304-342-2642
food stamps, mo (no min)

WISCONSIN
Indian Groceries and Spices
10633 West North Ave
Wauwatosa, WI 53226
414-771-3535
mo (no min, catalog)

CANADA

BRITISH COLUMBIA
J and B Foods
6607 Main St.
Vancouver, BC V5X 3H3
604-321-0224

Michael's Discount Foods
4169 Main St
Vancouver, BC V5V 3P6
Tel: 604-874-7912, Fax: 604-276-1610

MANITOBA
Dino's Grocery Mart
460 Notre Dame
Winnipeg, MB R3B 1R5
Tel & Fax: 204-942-1526
Visa, mo ($25 min)

VIP Supermarket
739 Ellice Ave
Winnipeg, MB R3G 0B5
Tel: 204-774-8671, Fax: 204-786-6213

NEWFOUNDLAND
India Gate Restaurant/Grocery
286 Duckworth St
St. Johns, NF A1C 1G9
709-753-6006
MC, Visa, Amex, mo ($75 min)
groceries ONLY from 5-6:30 PM

NOVA SCOTIA
India Groceries
2585 Robie St.
Halifax, NS B3K 4N5
902-423-6339
mo ($30 min)

ONTARIO
Indian Groceries and Spices
724 Wilson Ave
Downview, ON M3K 1E2
Tel & Fax: 416-630-4335
mo (COD)

India Bazaar
2645 Islington Ave
Islington, ON M9V 2X6
Tel: 416-749-0505, Fax: 416-749-6560
Visa, mo ($50 min)

Ganga Store
496 Kerr St
Oakville, ON
905-842-0126
mo (with s&h)

Daya Indian Grocery & Hlth Foods
8236 Young St
Thornhill, ON L4J 1W6
Tel: 905-881-0454, Fax: 905-881-0009
MC, Visa, mo ($50 min)

Kohinooor Foods
1438 Gerrard St. E
Toronto, ON M4L 1Z8
Tel & Fax: 416-461-4432
Visa, mo (no min)

Jane Food Store
1792 Jane St
Weston, ON M9N 2T2
Tel: 416-241-7486, Fax: 416-244-9173
mo ($100 min, flyer)

QUEBEC
Ram Das Foods, Ltd.
1501 Dollard
Ville LaSalle, PQ H8N 1T3
514-364-3817
Visa

SASKACHTEWAN
India Food Center
1213 15th Ave
Regina, SK S4P 0Y8
306-757-9940

Index

Index by Main Ingredient

Ask your store to carry these books, or you may order directly from:

The Book Publishing Company
P.O. Box 99
Summertown, TN 38483

Or call: 1-800-695-2241
Please add $2.50 per book for shipping

Almost-No Fat Cookbook	$10.95
American Harvest	11.95
Burgers 'n Fries 'n Cinnamon Buns	6.95
Cookin' Healthy with One Foot Out the Door	8.95
Cooking with Gluten and Seitan	7.95
Ecological Cooking: Recipes to Save the Planet	10.95
Fabulous Beans	9.95
From A Traditional Greek Kitchen	9.95
Good Time Eatin' in Cajun Country	9.95
George Bernard Shaw Vegetarian Cookbook	8.95
Holiday Diet Book	9.95
Indian Vegetarian Cooking at Your House	12.95
Instead of Chicken, Instead of Turkey	9.95
Judy Brown's Guide to Natural Foods Cooking	10.95
Kids Can Cook	9.95
Murrieta Hot Springs Vegetarian Cookbook	9.95
New Farm Vegetarian Cookbook	8.95
Now & Zen Epicure	17.95
Olive Oil Cookery	11.95
Peaceful Cook	8.95
Physician's Slimming Guide, Neal D. Barnard, M.D.	5.95
Also by Dr. Barnard:	
Foods That Cause You To Lose Weight	12.95
Live Longer, Live Better (90 min. cassette)	9.95
Shiitake Way	7.95
Shoshoni Cookbook	12.95
Simply Heavenly	19.95
The Sprout Garden	8.95
Starting Over: Learning to Cook with Natural Foods	10.95
Tempeh Cookbook	10.95
Ten Talents (Vegetarian Cookbook)	18.95
Tofu Cookery	14.95
Tofu Quick & Easy	7.95
TVP® Cookbook	6.95
Uncheese Cookbook	11.95
Uprisings: The Whole Grain Bakers' Book	13.95
Vegetarian Cooking for People with Diabetes	10.95